A Better Life

AN ITALIAN IMMIGRANT'S JOURNEY

as written by
Karen Guest

2020 Australia

Copyright © 2020 by Karen Guest.

All rights reserved. No part of this publication may be reproduced, distributed or transmitted in any form or by any means, including photocopying, recording, or other electronic or mechanical methods, without the prior written permission of the publisher, except in the case of brief quotations embodied in critical reviews and certain other noncommercial uses permitted by copyright law. For permission requests, write to the publisher at the address below.

Karen Guest, PO Box 1946, Sunnybank Hills, Queensland, Australia 4109

www.karenguest.com.au

Editor Julie Athanasiou

First published 2020

ISBN 978-0-9944663-2-7 (paperback)

Contents

Introduction 1
Life in Italy 5
The War Years 11
Thoughts of a Better Life 21
The Lucky Country 33
Catching Rabbits 45
Cutting Sugar Cane 51
Farming Life at Millaroo 59
Growing Tobacco 73
Sugar Cane Farming 89
Family 97
Losing Bruno 101
Building a Portfolio 109
Friendships 115
Second Chances 121
A Better Life 127
Italians in Australia 131

For Umberto and Anna

Dream as if you'll live forever,
live as if you'll die today.

—JAMES DEAN

Introduction

HAVE YOU EVER THOUGHT about what it might be like to migrate to another country? With the inevitable language and cultural differences, the life of an immigrant is not an easy path. Nonetheless, there have been many who have been courageous enough. The result can be most fulfilling for those who dare to dream of a better life.

This story is about Umberto, an Italian immigrant to Australia, who I met several years ago through my partner's family. Since then I have come to know him and his wife Anna, and a few years later her family, when we spent our holidays in Canada.

When Umberto and I first discussed writing his story, I was excited as I thought I understood what it was like to be an immigrant. After all, my family emigrated to Australia and based on what I knew about my own family, I felt I knew what it was like for him. I figured I knew the courage required and what it might have taken to make such a move. How wrong I was. It wasn't long before I realised I had no idea about the strength of character it would take to leave your family behind and start a new life on the other side of the world in a country where English was not your first language, and culturally, all that you knew was changed.

There is no doubt that despite the difficulties Umberto faced, he has lived a full life. How he came to be in Australia, his experience as a farmer and a property developer and what his life is like now has been a remarkable journey.

Umberto's courage is a testament to his determination and dreams of a better life. As we talked about his life, there was nothing that could have prepared me for what I was going to learn about his past. As he shared his journey, which began during the tumultuous times of the Second World War, it was hard at times not to cry, but ultimately it is a story about a boy who dreamt of a better life — and who succeeded in achieving that dream.

Umberto was born in a small country town in the historic village of Sezze in Southern Italy. Like many other children of his era, he was forced to grow up quickly; and well before becoming an adult, he was doing things and taking on responsibilities that would make the average person shudder in disbelief.

This story starts with the determination of a child who lived through the Great Depression and suffered from the effects of the Second World War. As a mother, I have struggled to come to terms with what his childhood would have been like during these difficult and uncertain times. From his earliest memories, Umberto recalled he strived to do better in everything he did and had a dream for a better life.

During the Second World War, Umberto's father was a prisoner of war, and for a long time, Umberto didn't know where he was. I cannot imagine how any child would cope with that and don't know how I would have felt. I can imagine many families experienced this during the war years. If that was not enough, Umberto's family home was seized by the German military, forcing them to live elsewhere.

I must admit I found it challenging to comprehend what it must have been like to sit on the knee of a German soldier, to hide from the Nazis, to hear gunfire and see tracer bullets in the night sky.

Umberto was an energetic, intelligent and determined child. As an 11-year-old, he started a wood collection business that made a small amount of money to help his family get through the cold winter months. This was not an easy thing for him to do, but even in the face of adversity, Umberto kept dreaming. He held his dreams alive and found the courage to make a change when the opportunity arose.

As a young adult, he chose to migrate to the other side of the world, rather than continue to live in the country in which he was born. With no expectations about what the future might bring, he went in search of a better life in Australia where he was initially humiliated and treated with suspicion. Even with the inevitable struggles of learning a new language, and taking on any job he could find, he was taught how to catch rabbits before working as a sugar cane cutter in the harsh conditions of North Queensland.

Eventually, his tenacity and incredibly hard work ethic led him to become a farmer and grew tobacco and sugar cane, before building an impressive residential and commercial property portfolio. He embraced the challenges and opportunities presented to him and always held true to his dreams in his adopted Australian home.

This very emotional story is a glimpse into some of the darkest and tumultuous times in history. It is also about a boy who against the odds grew into a compassionate, generous, determined, and somewhat stubborn man, who always dreamt of a better life, not only for himself but for others around him. As you follow Umberto on his journey, I hope you are captivated by the openness and honesty of his story. You may also find yourself curious about your heritage, where you have come from, how you happened to be here, and your journey through life.

It is sobering to know that while Umberto lived this life, I struggled to find the courage to keep listening. I wanted to write his story and to share it with others, but I knew it was going to be difficult. Even so, this is what Umberto wants; for his story to be told and for history, and his story, not to be forgotten.

CHAPTER 1

Life in Italy

THE GREAT DEPRESSION OF the 1930s was an unprecedented economic recession that had long-lasting effects for many countries across the world. For countless people, including those in Italy, it was a time when finding somewhere safe and warm to sleep and scavenging for food were accepted as everyday life. There is no denying those who lived through the Depression suffered greatly and felt its impact for many years as they fought for their lives, and countries rebuilt their economies. While there has been a lot written into the history books about this time and the Second World War, this story focuses on the personal struggles that are rarely shared with others.

This extraordinary story begins before Umberto was born, when in 1932 Italy's fascist dictator, Benito Mussolini, built a new city called Littoria. Littoria is located more than 64c kilometres south-west of Rome in Southern Italy. The area was a swampy marsh, known locally as quadraso, which had been dried out to cope with the building of infrastructure and houses. The city of Littoria was the capital of the province of Littoria until 1947 when it became known as Latina. In the small nearby historic town of Sezze, 19 kilometres north-west of Latina, is where Umberto's parents, Julio and Maria, were born, grew up, married and raised their family.

The Romans, known for building fortresses, constructed Sezze in the fifth century. It is not surprising the Romans built Sezze high on a hill at almost 300 metres above sea level for protection from invasion. A maze of tunnels through the mountainous terrain has irrigated the gently sloping surrounding landscape. The adjacent undulating landscape is covered with some fruit-bearing orchards and native trees which the people harvested for housing timber and firewood. The local people consider Sezze and the surrounding area to be beautiful as the landscape has the characteristics of each of the seasons at any time of year.

Umberto's family had owned land in the area since the 1700s. The family-owned one hectare of land in one area and combined with other small parcels of land, this added up to around five hectares in and around Sezze. Umberto's family were considered middle-class as his grandfather had lived in America for two years building a solid financial base. When his grandfather returned to Italy in the early 1900s, he had saved enough to be able to build his home on the family land. Years later, Umberto's father, Julio, spent time building his own home nearby on the same property. Like most houses in the area, it was made primarily from rocks and bound together by a mixture of sand and burnt crushed rocks that cemented the rocks together.

Umberto's parents, Julio and Maria, had a source of pride about being born and raised in Sezze. There is little known about their childhood, although it is thought they had not travelled outside of Italy. As young adults, they married and stayed in Sezze to raise their family. Given the era, there is no doubt they faced many challenges and hardships in the first few years of their marriage.

It was not long before Julio and Maria had their first child, a boy named Ercole. A short time later their family grew with the birth of Umberto during the coldest of winters in December 1932. In the years that followed, they had two more children, a boy named Ezio and a girl named Santina. They had a happy family life, a good income from subsistence farming, and the children enjoyed helping with chores on the farm. At the time and like many of their neighbours, they would not have known their lives would change during the coming years of the Depression and the Second World War.

Like many other families in and around Sezze, Umberto's family led a simple life and were primarily subsistence farmers, although they earned a good living selling their excess produce to manufacturers and other local families. This way of life was challenging due to the physical demands and total reliance on their crops reaching maturity. However, this had been their family's way of life for generations. There is no doubt they were fortunate as they grew a variety of crops, including tomatoes, garlic and onion, all used in cooking their daily meals as well suitable for bottling and long-term storage.

Julio and Maria produced almost everything they needed from an enormous variety of plants and fruit trees and were also nurturing a mature olive orchard. They were luckier than most other families and only had to buy salt, tobacco, matches and sugar from the local grocery store. They worked particularly hard to grow their wheat crops as it was a valuable commodity they could use for bartering. With one local manufacturer, they would exchange a medium size bag of flour, which they ground, for two pounds of handmade pasta. Their olive trees produced abundant fruit, and through discussions with the local mill, they exchanged boxes of olives for cooking oil.

The grapevines provided a reliable source of income as they made more than 20,000 litres of wine each year. As they were known for making good quality red wine, they quickly sold it to other families in the area. They also raised farm animals, including pigs, which were much sought after. Twice a year, some of the pigs were slaughtered for the meat which they shared with local families to make small goods, including prosciutto, which is a raw dry-cured ham that is thinly sliced and considered by some to be delicious.

Umberto's parents felt that raising their children on a farm was a great way to teach them about the benefits of farm life and how they could make a good living off the land. However, a tragedy occurred that had a profound impact on their family and changed the way they lived.

Their daughter Santina had been sick for some time before the doctor diagnosed a hernia. In those days, access to adequate health care was problematic. Santina, at just four-and-a-half years old, passed away unexpectedly from complications associated with the hernia. While Umberto and his family struggled with their personal loss, many others across the world were facing the implications of a world at war.

CHAPTER 2

The War Years

IN THE AUTUMN OF 1939, when the Second World War broke out, Umberto was seven years old and in Grade Four at a local school. While he did not understand what was happening, he knew that things had changed as many local people were being forced out of their homes. Family life on the farm was now very different.

In the early days of the war, Italy aligned itself with Germany against the rest of the world. As things rapidly changed, and as Germany invaded Italy, they took over Umberto's hometown of Sezze and before long Umberto's family home. As it happened in many parts of the world, the Germans destroyed buildings and farms, confiscated the use of private homes and guarded significant infrastructure, including bridges.

During the 1940s in Italy, mandatory national service become law requiring men of a certain age to enlist in the military. When this happened, families either collapsed and dispersed from the stress or consolidated and came together. It was a swift process when the government called upon the men in the household to enlist in the army. There was no choice as they had to join the military or be branded a deserter and imprisoned.

At the time, the only exception to avoid national service where if there were four children in the family. Julio and Maria knew that had Umberto's sister, Santina, survived, Julio would not have been forced into the army. Julio entered compulsory national service and life continued and moved on ever so slowly. Like most children whose fathers were in national service, Umberto missed his father and was forced to grow up quickly under challenging circumstances.

By 1943 Umberto's education had been suspended. There was no discussing it with his mother, but during these challenging and uncertain times, 11-year-old Umberto felt he had to be strong, which meant working to bring in extra money for his family.

The sense of community in Umberto's hometown of Sezze started to change for the worse. It was the first time that Italian men had been forced to enlist for national service. Not only that, with no experience, they were forced to learn to fly aeroplanes and gliders at the local civilian airfield as part of the war effort. Even though there were only a few aircraft available, it was not long before the government ultimately took over the operation of the airfield. Just nearby in the lower part of Sezze, there was a base training camp for the new soldiers who learnt how to fly aeroplanes in very short timeframes, which they would often crash.

In September 1943, large numbers of families fled from their homes as the German army took over small towns like Sezze all over Italy. There was no doubt that if families had stayed in their homes, they would have been taken as prisoners of war and detained by the German military or even killed if they refused.

Not far from Umberto's home, the German military set up camp kitchens to prepare daily meals for their foot soldiers who were going back and forth to the front line. As time passed, Umberto came to understand what was happening and felt sad as family friends and neighbours went openly into the camp kitchens to beg for food so they could feed their families. However, there was no special treatment or meals made for the Italian families; they were only given the leftover food that had not been consumed by the German soldiers.

As the German soldiers moved into Sezze, and much to Umberto's family's dismay, their home was seized. They also confiscated their wheat crops which had been in storage in the drying shed on their property. For Umberto's family, this meant there was no flour or other food to sell to the local business or that they could share with other families. The Germans also took possession of the farm machinery and anything they could find to use for themselves or to salvage for parts for their own equipment.

The Germans not only took over Umberto's family home, but they also forced his family out into the cold and left them to fend for themselves. The German soldiers needed a base camp which was close to the front line and for ease of access so they could provide support for their military forces across Italy. From here the Germans marched back and forth to the front line from early in the morning until they returned in the early evening when another group of soldiers went to the front line.

Umberto's family were lucky enough to be able to stay with another family, who had not been displaced, just a short distance away. From here, they were able to watch the German soldiers at night in their former home through the windows into the brightly lit rooms.

As a curious child, Umberto would, at times, creep up to his family home to see what the soldiers were doing. On one occasion he climbed up onto an old, broken wooden crate outside an open window just near the kitchen. With his fingers clamped onto the windowsill, Umberto stood on his toes, stretching his tiny body high enough to be able to look in through the window.

As he looked around the kitchen, he saw some German soldiers talking. They seemed very dirty and were wearing their helmets, while their rifles were leaning up against the wall. Some of them were smoking, and as he stared at them, he caught the attention of one soldier who smiled at him, and he returned his smile.

"Young boy, what are you doing? Get down from the window and come here," the German soldier said.

The German soldier gestured with his hands to Umberto and then pointed for him to walk through the kitchen door towards him. While Umberto could not understand what the soldier said, he did what he thought the man wanted him to do. He clumsily climbed down from the wooden crate he was standing on, then straightened out his clothes, and took a deep breath before entering the kitchen.

"I won't hurt you. Come here," said the German soldier.

A Better Life

Unsure of what he was getting into, Umberto hung his head down as he slowly walked through the kitchen door and over to where this German soldier was sitting. With his tiny hands clenched into a fist, he walked toward the soldier who he felt meant him no harm from the soft tone of his voice. Umberto moved closer and still not knowing what would happen, he sat on the soldier's knee while the conversation continued.

"You remind me of my own child. We'll be friends. Okay?" said the German soldier.

Still, Umberto could not understand, although he did start feeling comfortable, so he just smiled. Over the next few weeks, Umberto ran back to the family home many times in the early evening to visit with this soldier. While neither of them could understand what each other was saying and Umberto did not even know his name, they still developed a relationship like that of a father and son. All he really knew was that he did not feel threatened by this soldier, even though he was one of many soldiers who had taken over his family home.

Umberto worked out he could see this soldier each time he returned from the frontline and so continued to visit for some time before it came to an abrupt stop. On one visit, Umberto wandered through his family home amongst the soldiers looking for the soldier who was his friend, but he could not find him.

"Young boy, our comrade, your friend, he has died from gunshot wounds," said another German soldier.

Umberto did not understand what was said or what had happened to his friend, but he knew by the tone of his voice that it was not good. He never saw this soldier again, although he did continue to visit the family home for as long as the war lasted hoping that he might see him.

Despite the war being at the village doorstep, Umberto was somewhat shielded from the atrocities; the time he spent with this soldier were happy times, and he could tell that the man enjoyed his visits as they laughed a lot together.

To Umberto, all the German soldiers looked the same. However, he was old enough to understand they did not all behave the same way. He also knew enough to know the soldier who befriended him was one of many German foot soldiers who did not hurt anyone in Sezze but had big heavy guns that shot bullets and could kill people. However, he felt there was something about the way they behaved, the way they dressed, and their authority that was very different to the other soldiers who often terrorised the people of Sezze in the streets and surrounding meeting places.

He came to know the other soldiers as the Nazis, the protection squads. He quickly understood enough to remember the Nazis were the evil ones. He felt this way because if someone did something wrong or were believed to be a spy, the Nazis would physically brand that person with a red-hot poker. It was well known that spies were dealt with and were also nearly always taken away to be shot and killed. All the children in Sezze clearly understood the difference between the foot soldiers and the Nazis and made sure they did not get caught up in any confrontation with them.

A Better Life

The Nazis were known to regularly travel through the same towns, including Sezze, capturing adults and children over the age of 14 years. As was often the case when the Nazis came to town, the adults, who were keeping watch, would tell the children to spread the word that the Nazis were coming so they would have time to hide. If this didn't happen, the Nazis would take them away, and they were never to be seen again.

The town of Sezze was in the second line of defence where the American soldiers used to shoot at the German soldiers. During the latter part of the war, the Americans landed at Asunatuno near the sea on the other side of Latina. Here there was a man-made channel called Canal Mussolini, about two or three kilometres from the beach, which was built to take the water out of the swamp so the land could be made suitable for building. It was here the American and German soldiers were on opposite sides of the channel fighting each other.

There were times when Umberto's family left Sezze for a few days to go to the mountains where at night it was like daylight due to the bombs going off and the shooting. Umberto watched as the tracer bullets from machine guns were visible as they tracked through the evening sky and lit up the surrounding countryside. Umberto and his brothers were young and did not feel scared, although they knew if bullets hit them, they could be killed.

When they walked along the roads during the day, if they came across an unexploded hand grenade or a landmine, they knew not to touch it as it could quickly blow up if moved. Even the bridges had mines, and because they knew where they were, were always cautious when crossing them. As there was so much ammunition laying on the ground, there were many times people found unexploded hand grenades and threw them in the river. The weapons would explode, and the fish floated to the surface and collected for food.

As a child living through a war, Umberto noticed that many things influenced what people did and how their lives changed. Families everywhere spent each day working out how to survive. When evening came, the nights were long for everyone — adults and children alike. Umberto would often hear the gunfire followed by the bullets exploding as they passed close by and above his head. The fighting often continued after sunset with the tracer bullets lighting up the sky so brightly, and for so long it was possible to read a newspaper or book.

IN FOCUS: ITALY DURING THE DEPRESSION AND SECOND WORLD WAR

The Great Depression (1929-1939) was the worst economic downturn in the history of the industrial world. It began after the stock market crash of October 1929, which sent Wall Street investors into a panic and wiping out millions of investment funds. Over the next few years, as consumer spending and investment dropped, there was a steep decline in industrial output and employment as companies laid-off workers to survive the economic downturn.

A Better Life

Italy was an impoverished nation in comparison to France and Britain. However, Italy's fascist dictator, Benito Mussolini, wanted to advance Italy's economy and pursued battles for the land, lira and grain. The struggle for land saw marshland cleared, making it usable for farming and housing. The battle of the lira was to restore the purchasing power from bygone days. The struggle for grain was about growing grain crops at the expense of fruit and vegetables, which failed as Italy's economic base was small and was primarily an agricultural economy.

The Second World War followed the Depression, the leading cause being the rise of the Nazi Party in Germany and its invasion of other countries. Linked to the First World War, the Nazi Party filled a gap that brought the country out of its depression. To do this, they blamed marginalised groups, such as the Jewish citizens, and was the beginning of the Holocaust. Germany pushed into surrounding countries, including Austria and Czechoslovakia, officially starting the Second World War when they invaded Poland on 1 September 1939.

The European nations led by Great Britain and France hoped that by allowing Adolf Hitler, Germany's dictator, to have additional territory, they could avoid war. Hitler, however, saw the concessions as a sign of weakness and continued his conquest of Europe.

Italy joined the Second World War as an ally of Germany in 1940, by order of its dictator, Benito Mussolini. Mussolini had territorial and imperial ambitions of his own and saw allying with Germany as a chance to achieve his goals.

When Italy joined the war, fighting between Germany and the Allies had already moved too far north for the Italians to have an impact, although it did bring the war to the Mediterranean region. Italy invaded British-occupied North Africa and Greece without informing Germany, which required Germany's intervention with troops it needed elsewhere.

Germany took over Yugoslavia in 1941 to get to Greece to help the Italians. After the Allies took over Sicily, the Italian leaders deposed Mussolini, withdrew from the alliance with Germany and signed a peace treaty with the Allies.

The United States entered the Second World War in December 1941, by declaring war on Japan for bombing the United States naval base at Pearl Harbor and then joined the war in Europe. The Allied countries fought a grueling campaign to force the German troops out of Italy with the Second World War coming to an end in 1945.

CHAPTER 3

Thoughts of a Better Life

WHILE UMBERTO DID NOT fully comprehend what was happening around him as a child, as far as he can remember, he always had the idea to work on improving himself to prepare for a better future. Even as a young child, it was this dream that helped him to embrace the opportunities that came his way.

Umberto's family was no different from many other families during and after the Second World War in that they regularly had to do things they would not usually have done to survive.

By 1943 the German military had captured Italy and along the way had destroyed much of the country's infrastructure. The locals scavenged whatever they could and what they did not need, and then sold what they could to buy clothing and food for their families. The local airport in Sezze had been destroyed and become a dumping ground for unusable aeroplanes and other wreckage that had been left to deteriorate. It was a deliberate reminder that Italy had been taken over by the Germans and they weren't in a hurry to clean up the mess they had created.

Around this time, Umberto's father was arrested by the French government and taken as a prisoner of war. He was transported to Algeria in Northern Africa for internment. With his father absent, Umberto's mother consistently worked hard to keep the family safe from the German military and to keep food on the table for her children.

The local grocery store in Sezze was located near Umberto's family home and stocked most of the basic food supplies and household products the locals needed. The grocery store was in an old building and was in significant disrepair due to the impact of the war.

The food supplies included staples such as pasta, flour, olives and bread as well as wood chips used for heating and cooking. However, the store did not sell salt or tobacco, which was in demand, as this was often in short supply and difficult to obtain during the war years. Even though people needed to buy products from the store, their resources were meagre, resulting in the store not being able to sell enough of its products to make a profit.

Umberto was a resourceful child and was always looking for ways to make extra money to help his family. He came up with what he thought was a great idea to gather and sell wood in opposition to the grocery store. The plan revolved around him sourcing and collecting firewood and selling it to friends and others who lived in the local community. However, he did not quite know how he would do this.

One day, as Umberto walked down the road past the grocery store, he met his friend Cesere who was sitting on the side of the road. They had not seen each other for a while, and after a general catch up, Umberto discussed his plan to gather and sell wood, and it turned out that Cesere had an idea that could help him. They stood and spoke for some time and discussed how Umberto could build a cart to transport the wood he was proposing to collect and resell.

"Umberto, I found some things from a crashed aeroplane from over there. Want to see?" said Cesere.

"Show me," said Umberto.

Cesere took Umberto to a where an aeroplane had crashed on the other side of the field and pointed to where the wheels were. Now, Umberto was smart enough to know that Cesere didn't own the planes. However, he decided to listen to his sales pitch as he was hoping there were some wheels he could use for his wooden cart.

"There are lots of parts of these planes that can be easily adapted to other things. I want to sell them," said Cesere.

Umberto was very impressed with Cesere's stash and quietly smiled to himself as he looked around the wrecked aeroplanes. Cesere had found two reasonably good wheels that he could use for building a wooden cart to transport the wood he was planning to collect and sell to the public. Umberto was quite excited about the prospect of creating his cart sooner rather than later as it meant he could make money quickly and help his family.

"I want to buy those two wheels. How much?" said Umberto.

"One Lire," said Cesere smiling.

Umberto took off his gloves, reached into his pocket and pulled out one Lire which he promptly handed over to Cesere. The deal was done. Umberto picked up the wheels and rolled them home; along the way looked for other materials he could use. It was not long before Umberto saw some discarded timber outside an abandoned shed, and although a bit rough, the wood was decent enough to use in constructing the wooden cart.

After getting the wheels home, he returned to the shed and dragged some of the wood to his home so he could commence building as quickly as possible.

It took him several days out in the cold to build the cart; he struggled with the simple construction in the freezing conditions. Eventually, after a few failed attempts, he finally finished it.

The cart had a roughly flat wooden base and sidebars to safeguard the wheels and two wooden harnesses which sat on the axles. Umberto also added long wooden handles to prevent it from tipping over as he dragged it around. His plan was nearly a reality.

Umberto did not think that sourcing the wood for his new business adventure would be an issue. However, it would prove to be another hurdle. He spent some time searching locally around the town for sources of wood in the backyards of local houses and on the edges of town. He eventually heard from friends that there was a group of people clearing the wooded areas on the far outskirts of Sezze in the surrounding forest.

It took Umberto an hour in the bitter cold to drag his cart through the snow away from the town and over the bumpy ground to the area where the people were working. He noticed the trees these people were cutting down were quite dense and had easy-to-cut thick branches, making it the perfect wood to burn in a fireplace. He knew immediately this was the wood he wanted and that it would be easy to sell for the extra money he needed. He left his cart and walked over to where the people were working and talk with them about what he wanted.

"Hello, could you please stop so we could talk?" said Umberto.

"Yes, son, what is it?" said the man.

"Could I buy some branches from you?" said Umberto.

"Why?" said the man.

"I want to sell the branches to make some extra money," said Umberto.

"If you think you can, of course," said the man.

"Will you just sell to me, no one else? Please?" said Umberto.

"Well, that would be ok," said the man.

As it happened, Umberto was the only person who had been able to secure such an arrangement with this group of people. As soon as he could, Umberto set about collecting, stacking and bundling the wood, which was backbreaking work for a child — even more so in the cold conditions.

Once Umberto paid the group of people, he carried the wood bundles on his shoulders for nearly a mile to where he had left the cart with his body aching from the hard work. Collecting and loading the wood by himself often took many hours. He then pulled it along the cobblestone road for almost a further two miles to reach the other side of town. From here, it was just a few hundred feet to his home.

Umberto's fingers were often blue from the cold as he dragged his cart around the local streets. He would sell his wood along the local roads and often to his neighbours for their oversized wood fire ovens. It was not unexpected that he quickly got to know who those people were because they baked their bread in much bigger ovens than the standard family oven, and they would give him food to take home for his family. Although this was hard work for a young child, Umberto felt he achieved great things by helping his family.

At one stage, it was a shock to many of the locals that the grocery store almost closed because Umberto was selling so much wood elsewhere for less. The storekeeper did not hold anything against Umberto, although he also had to make a profit.

By selling wood this way, Umberto made a good profit. He was lucky to be able to buy a bundle of timber for 15 lire and to resell it for 25 lire, quite a good return for anyone, let alone a child. Umberto was very proud of his ability to make a profit in this way as he was helping his family to survive.

As the war continued, life went on in Italy, albeit in a different way for many families. Eventually, the American military forces arrived and started pushing the German military on the front line back from where they came. In 1945, within eight months of the American military's arrival, the end of the war came quickly when Germany officially surrendered to the Allies.

Umberto continued to work in his wood supply business until mid-1946 when his father was released from prison and made his way back home. Umberto's family was pleased to have their husband and father back at home. Umberto's father was impressed with what Umberto had been doing to build a wood supply business to help the

A Better Life

family. However, it was not long before Umberto's father was able to again help his family in ways that he had not been able to do for many years through working on the family land and growing crops.

Soon after Umberto's father's arrival back in Italy, Julio arranged for Umberto to start school again and continue his education. He finished in 1950 at 18 years of age.

As there was little work available, Umberto immediately started working on the land with his father. This was expected of him and was the case for many subsistence farming families. Unfortunately, Umberto felt there was not a great future in doing so, but opportunities to do other things were limited.

Due to the war, Italy's economy was in tatters, while the damage to the infrastructure was so extensive some areas needed a massive rebuild. It was hard for many people to see why there was so little work available for young men looking for a job under such circumstances considering that there was significant infrastructure needing repair.

At this time many people from war-torn Europe had begun emigrating to other countries in search of a better life. It was not long before Umberto became restless, and an opportunity arose that would change his life.

Initially, Umberto decided to apply to join the Navy or the Police Force. As he waited for a response, government policies changed, permitting Italians an opportunity to emigrate to another country. Thousands of Italians decided to migrate as there were so few jobs available in their home country.

In an unprecedented move, the Australian government extended invitations to Italian citizens between the ages of 18 and 32 to migrate to Australia. With as much excitement as there was trepidation, Umberto decided to apply for migration to some countries, including Australia. He did not mind where he was going, just that he could go.

Umberto decided to accept the first offer he received and waited patiently for any news. It was a nerve-wracking wait as he felt this was his only chance at a better life. Even though this opportunity could be on the other side of the world, Umberto decided he was going to take the chance.

To be considered as a migrant, any applicant who was 33 years old or older, was automatically rejected by the authorities. Although this age requirement did not affect Umberto, all applicants were put under tremendous scrutiny as part of the application process. In addition to the age barrier, applicants had to be single, fit and healthy. The exception was if an applicant had family in Australia already, in which case they were accepted without question. There was also a political checking process which meant if an applicant had an association with the wrong political party, they would not be selected for migration with no opportunity to recant and have the decision overturned.

Australia was the first country to make an offer of placement for Umberto to migrate. Before he knew it, he was packing and preparing to leave his family and friends behind. The only things he needed to take were his clothes and a few personal items, all of which fitted into a small number of suitcases.

A Better Life

The trip to Australia by boat would cost £96, which was out of reach for most Italians. The Australian government made an offer of a loan for passage, although there were some strings attached. The government required migrants to pay back the loan at the rate of £4 per month over two years, negating the need for upfront payment. They also needed to pay a one-off fee of 14,000 lire before leaving Italy which the Australian government claimed would help them once they arrived in Australia.

The Australian government had a plan for new immigrants. This plan included giving them an unemployment benefit, so they had some money to help with the costs of starting life in a new country. The one-off payment was primarily in the form of an unemployment benefit with an amount deducted for accommodation and food, resulting in a balance of four shillings per week for other living expenses.

Packed and ready to go, the day came when Umberto was due to leave Italy for an unknown future on the other side of the world. It was a sad day for his family as they travelled with him to the Port of Naples (Napoli) in the Campania region of Southern Italy where he boarded a large passenger ship to start his adventure. There were emotional scenes at the dock as he waved goodbye to his family who thought they would never see him again.

The ship was called the Hellenic Prince, initially constructed in 1924 called the HMAS Albatross that the Royal Australian Navy used as a seaplane carrier. The most important service the ship was involved with was the Normandy landings in France where it was attacked by enemy aircraft and hit by a torpedo. After some time, the boat was eventually repurposed and converted to bring displaced persons to Australia and renamed. It turned out the ship was the only Australian-built ship to bring migrants to Australia.

On this voyage, there were thousands of people on board, although the only females were from Greece and Turkey. There were more than 900 men from Italy, with most unable to speak English, although Umberto did meet two people who had been to Australia before. These two men had been in Africa between 1943 and 1945 when Italy was fighting the Australians at war; they had been taken as prisoners of war and transported to Australia for internment. With this call for migrants, they had been accepted to migrate to go back to Australia to work for the farmers they worked for previously.

The Italian men shared cabins, which could hold up to two, four and six people. Umberto was fortunate to be able to share with three other men and had easy access inside the cabin to the bathroom and toilet facilities. The treatment they received on board was excellent, and due to the efforts of an Italian chef, they had good food and plenty of it, with everyone putting on weight as a result.

After 29 days at sea, the Hellenic Prince arrived on the west coast of Australia on 6 July 1952. Umberto had made it. This was meant to be the beginning of Umberto's new adventure and a better life in Australia. Little did he know at the time how he would be treated by a country that had asked him to come and resettle.

A Better Life

***

IN FOCUS: THE DEPRESSION AND MIGRATION IN AUSTRALIA

The Great Depression was a time of extreme hardship for many people in Australia and across the world. The period began before the unprecedented market crash in prices and lasted until the end of the Second World War. Unemployment in Australia more than doubled to twenty-one per cent in mid-1930 and reached its peak in mid-1932 when almost thirty-two per cent of Australians were out of work.

The impact on Australian society was devastating. Without work and a steady income, many people lost their homes and were forced to live in makeshift dwellings with inadequate heating and sanitation. Other social consequences included working-class teenage children consistently leaving school, and married women carrying a more significant domestic burden.

Migrants, particularly those from Italy and southern Europe, were resented because they worked for less wages than others despite having relatively little in the way of family or friends to call on for help.

CHAPTER 4

The Lucky Country

LOOKING BACK ON HIS life in the Sezze in Southern Italy, Umberto feels the impact of the Second World War had a significant impact not only on himself but on those who continued to live there. It is also likely the emotional impact would have haunted those who chose to move away to other parts of the world for many years. However, Umberto held a firm belief in himself and his dream of a better life and so decided he would take on the challenges that Australia, the lucky country, would inevitably bring him.

Some say Umberto turned his back on his home country, yet he felt there was nothing for him there. Many other Europeans must have felt as Umberto did as demonstrated by the exodus of people to other countries. In his heart, Umberto felt the right thing for him was to make a new life somewhere else. Because of this, he accepted the offer to go to Australia and never wavered in his dream for a better life.

When the Hellenic Prince docked at the port in Freemantle, just south of Perth, Freemantle was a bustling market town. The primary wholesale markets were selling an eclectic mix of fresh produce and products, reflective of the many different migrants who settled there. It was no surprise then that the Hellenic Prince had cargo to deliver and no doubt other freight headed for private destinations.

On arriving at the port in Freemantle, Umberto felt a sense of pride that he had made it to Australia. Without much fanfare and quite unexpectedly, Umberto and the other passengers were permitted to disembark and were able to spend the day in town. However, he did not see much as he just wandered through the markets with the friends he had made on the ship. As Umberto walked around, there were vast amounts of beautiful fruit, including oranges, apples and pears, the likes of which he had not seen for a long time. They all looked delicious, so he bought a few pieces of fruit to take with him on the ship as it continued its journey.

By the end of the day, more than 300 of the ship's passengers did not return to the Hellenic Prince. Umberto was not surprised that so many decided to make Freemantle their home. However, he wanted to continue his journey and returned to the ship. Once all the continuing passengers were on board, the Hellenic Prince set sail for Melbourne. As the ship departed, there were many emotional scenes as the people who stayed behind waved goodbye from the docks to those who remained on the ship.

It took an additional seven days to reach Melbourne, albeit with some controversy. On the way, the ship hit the ocean bed in just seven feet of water. However, before being grounded, it quickly backed away and continued its journey into deeper water. Even though they were close to

A Better Life

Melbourne, another ship from Italy, the La Napoli, also transporting immigrants to Australia, sailed alongside them over the next few days.

After the ship docked at the Port of Melbourne, and for some time, none of the passengers knew that the ship's hull was cracked, or that there had been concerns over it sinking. In hindsight, Umberto had felt uneasy on the last part of the trip as it was rough; so rough at times he thought the ship could have sunk.

After waiting for many hours, Umberto was getting ready to disembark. However, he and many others were not prepared for the treatment they were about to experience. Despite freely disembarking in Freemantle, in Melbourne, the Italians were prevented from leaving the ship and directed to go to another floor. They could see people from Greece and Turkey were walking freely off the ship, with some reuniting with people who had been waiting for them. However, the treatment the Italians received was entirely different, and they did not understand what was happening.

"You Italians, go that way. Follow the signs. You are not allowed to leave the ship," shouted the immigration official.

Most of the Italians could not speak English or understand what was going on. There was a lot of confusion amongst them as they knew they were being shouted at, although some translators arrived and were able to help.

The immigration official gestured with his hands for the Italians to follow staff who were leading them to another area. The people Umberto knew who could speak English began to spread the word about what they had to do. It turned out they were being moved back to their cabins to shower before going down the stairwells to a massive room at the bottom of the boat that smelt like dead fish.

None of the Italian men could understand why they were being treated differently to the people from Greece or Turkey. Just as they were talking amongst themselves to see what they could do; they heard another immigration official shouting at people on the other side of the room.

"You Italians take off your clothes — everything. Then place your clothes with your suitcases."

Umberto did not understand what was happening as he could not speak English, but the authorities made it clear what they expected by pulling at their clothes. As they were all men, undressing was not a huge issue, although it was not how he thought he should be treated.

They quickly realised they had no choice. Once undressed, the Italians were disinfected with a wet spray while their clothing and belongings were fumigated. Umberto and some of the others were angry and humiliated about their treatment and hugely disappointed. They felt the treatment they received was offensive and wondered if it was a taste of what was to come.

Before disembarking, they had to be physically assessed once again by Australian medical staff before being given clearance to go ashore. Due to the scrutiny during the application process in Italy, it was unlikely for officials to reject anyone for migration, except if they had done something wrong. The medical staff inspected their mouths, teeth, and eyes. The physical examination was a slow process and could not be escaped as you had to be 100 per cent physically fit to be allowed to leave the ship.

While it seemed to take an extraordinarily long time, they were eventually allowed to leave. Once Umberto and his friends disembarked, they were escorted onto waiting trains and transported to the Bonegilla Migrant Centre (Bonegilla). Although they did not realise this at the time, Bonegilla was nearly 200 miles away in a rural location, and initially constructed to accommodate prisoners during the Second World War.

Upon arrival, as Umberto wandered around, he thought there might be about 15,000 other immigrants as well as those who had just arrived. The rumours around Bonegilla were that the immigrants were prisoners of the government and not allowed to leave unless they had a job. To their surprise, there were many other things the immigrants had to accept and get used to in their newly adopted homeland.

Umberto did not quite know what to think now that he was in Australia. It did not take long for him to wonder if migrating was a huge mistake, but he did not know how to move on. However, after contemplating his future and dealing with emotions, Umberto remembered where he had come from, and the thoughts of his dream for a better life came alive again. He knew that living in Bonegilla was going to be difficult, although accepted things as they were.

There was no doubt there were some challenges to overcome; the first was not starving to death as the food provided was not good. It was nothing like it was back in Italy or on the ship. The food prepared for them included boiled mutton and pasta made by Yugoslavian cooks employed at Bonegilla, and it was clear they did not understand, care or considered the needs of the Italian people. Umberto remembers the pasta was like cement and so gluey that if a handful were thrown against the wall, it would stick. Also, the bread was not like the panini they were used to eating back in Italy.

Each day was the same for Umberto and many others at Bonegilla. Umberto was an early riser and managed to get through each day by eating as many boiled eggs and cheese as he could at breakfast. This was not easy to do, and he still lost weight and dropped 13kg down to 55kg in the short time he was a resident in Bonegilla.

The quality of the food was generally an issue for many of the Italian people. They found it frustrating to know there was also not much they could do about it as the administrators made it clear that nothing would change. Making the best of things was something that Umberto strived to do, no matter what the circumstance.

The living conditions in the accommodation blocks were basic and of timber construction with iron roofs, and the inside walls lined with a type of chipboard that looked like wood and sort of kept out the cold. Umberto recalls there were around 16 camps in Bonegilla and up to one thousand people living in each section. The accommodation blocks for single people consisted of one room each and was in a different part to the accommodation blocks for family groups. The family accommodation blocks comprised of two or three bedrooms. Umberto shared a room with three other men. There were four single beds in the room, and they shared bathroom facilities with others in a different building.

The government considered that one of the most significant opportunities for newly arrived migrants was being able to understand the English language enough to get by without being taken advantage.

For Umberto, who could not speak English, he knew there was a considerable challenge ahead of him. He had heard through friends that there were English classes offered at Bonegilla. However, at the time, he did not take up the offer as he did not plan on being there long enough to do so.

Without any knowledge of the English language, any work undertaking was a significant challenge. In talking about his experience at Bonegilla, Umberto said: "I felt as though I was in prison and treated the same as a prisoner of war."

Umberto realised very early on that if he was to have a better life, he had to secure employment outside of the camp. He thought about this almost every day and was always looking for opportunities that would help him leave.

After settling in and making friends, there was nothing much to do except to find a way to accept everything and get through each day without too much stress. Umberto did not smoke, drink or play cards, so he spent a lot of time sitting around talking with his new friends, although some people were playing soccer.

A Spanish man, who was residing at Bonegilla, shot himself in a desperate bid to be released. While this was a shock to Umberto, he could not help but feel he came to Australia for a better life and still held that dream close to his heart.

After a few days, Umberto received some news about his cousin, Gino, who had arrived in Australia some four months earlier. Gino was one of the lucky ones who quickly secured employment outside of the camp. Umberto wrote to Gino asking him to ask his boss for a job that would enable him to leave.

It was just a few days later when Umberto heard that Gino's boss had agreed to hire him. He was thrilled. Some 28-long, tiring and frustrating days after arriving at Bonegilla, Umberto left to start work with his cousin in an area that was hundreds of miles in the opposite direction to where he had first arrived in Australia. His journey for a better life was about to move at a much faster pace.

Umberto knew it was going to be a challenge to make his way to his new employer. As Umberto could not speak English, special arrangements were made for him. These arrangments included someone from Bonegilla taking him to the bus stop, where he waited for the bus to arrive in the heat of the midday sun. Once the bus came, Umberto sat patiently as it travelled along the highway into Melbourne. When he arrived in Melbourne, someone was waiting to take him to his hotel. Umberto was most gracious; there was always someone attending to him.

A Better Life

After a long day of travelling, Umberto finally arrived at the farm where his cousin was working. Upon arriving at the farm, Umberto did not waste any time and went to work straight away by helping the workers with the chores. The owners of the farm quickly realised he could not speak much English, so they initially showed him what to do using gestures.

A few days after starting work with his cousin, he had heard the Bonegilla residents had staged a revolution against being held captive. The newspapers reported it, and although he could not read it, his friends wrote to him about what happened. It was published in the papers that Bonegilla was taken over by the military who terrorised the residents with their machine guns. However, leaders who represented the various countries met with the Australian authorities who decided to set the residents free. The day after the revolution, the residents were free to leave. From there, they mostly went to Melbourne, although Umberto felt he was lucky to have already moved on.

Despite being shown what to do on the farm without the need for English, Umberto soon realised he would need to speak English if he was to find other work. To reach this goal, he completed an English course over the next few months by correspondence. The course was offered by a teacher who worked at Bonegilla, who was very kind to Umberto. The course involved them writing to each other each week in English, which forced Umberto to learn the language. Umberto also complemented this by attending the local high school with six other Italian men.

It took just seven months before Umberto could speak fluent English which greatly assisted him in the early days of being in Australia. Now that he could speak English, he felt the opportunities would present themselves to him. It was not much longer before his father wrote him a letter offering to pay for his fare back to Italy and return to life on the farm. However, returning to Italy was never going to be an option for Umberto as he had chosen Australia and never had any serious thoughts of returning to Italy.

Over time he learned to accept that his experience at Bonegilla was just a small part of the beginning of his journey. Working with Gino was a step forward, and he was now free to do as he pleased. Little did he know that there were so many opportunities ahead of him where he would need to make definitive choices if he was to make the best of his life in his newly adopted homeland.

***

IN FOCUS: THE BONEGILLA EXPERIENCE

In 1940, the military used the Bonegilla Camp in rural Victoria for training armed service personnel, and between 1944 and 1947 to hold Italian prisoners of war. After the Second World War and until 1951, the Bonegilla Migrant Reception and Training Centre (Bonegilla) was home to almost 170,000 migrants. In total, 320,000 migrants from 30 nations knew it as their first home until it closed in 1971.

The first migrants arrived at Bonegilla late in 1947 with transport, security and catering services provided by

A Better Life

the army. On arrival, the new migrants were allocated a hut and issued with utensils, crockery, towels and bedding. The living conditions were simple, and little was done to change the former army camp. The accommodation was harsh, with communal eating, washing and recreation facilities. Family members were separated, with men in one hut, single women in another, and women with children in another. The government did nothing to address the impact on families, although it was intended it be a place where they could catch their breath before becoming part of the Australian community.

The Australian government considered the new immigrants as a labour pool that would be crucial in the country's post-war reconstruction. Bonegilla was also the principal employment office assessing employability and sending migrants all over Australia, with some employed there for their first job. The non-British migrants learnt English and became familiar with a new way of life to assimilate into the broader Australian society. The new migrants knew Bonegilla to be Australia – along with the heat, the cold, the sun, the flies, the sense of isolation and barrenness.

Between 1949 and 1950 there was a surge in arrivals at Bonegilla. From 1951, Bonegilla received migrants and refugees and was primarily a staging camp providing temporary support and accommodation for new migrants who had exchanged free or assisted passage to Australia.

During the economic downturn between 1952 - 1961, some migrants held demonstrations demanding work and had cause to be unhappy. Many left employment in their homeland and emigrated to Australia and had been told work would be available. They felt they had been duped, leading to frustration and riots. In 1952, the army was called in, and in 1961 carloads of police, to curtail the violence.

Between 1960 and 1961, the German and Italian migrants again protested violently at not being allocated work and at the extended time spent in the Centre. The government introduced funding to improve the facilities although this ended up directed elsewhere. After this time, people from Indonesia and Czechoslovakia started arriving. Bonegilla closed its doors in 1971.

CHAPTER 5

Catching Rabbits

DURING THE 1950S IN Australia, one of life's complications for an Italian immigrant was prejudices affecting their employment. There was undoubtedly work available; however, finding the work was one thing and being allowed to do the job was another. For the young man who dreamed of a better life, Umberto's fortitude and determination kept his hopes alive as he tried different types of employment before taking a leap of faith and embracing every opportunity that presented itself. His decision to accept the job offers, contrary to the advice of others, changed his direction in life.

Umberto's first job in Australia was catching rabbits with his cousin Gino. He worked with three other Italians, an Indigenous man and the owner of the local cattle and sheep station where he was working. Umberto came to learn the station owner's received government subsidies when they hired labour to help destroy the rabbits. This was fortunate for Umberto as he worked there for several months, although not with the same people as the workers were transient and moved from job to job. While he knew the rabbits were a pest to the station owners and had to be destroyed, he also caught some for himself to supplement his daily diet.

In learning the trade, Umberto dug trenches with simple tools. He chased the female rabbits, including the babies, into the ditches with the sole purpose of burying them alive to kill them. The owner had 27 dogs available to chase the rabbits if they managed to run out of the trench. With the male rabbits, they would skin them and take them home and use them as a food supply. The station owner collected and sold the skins to a man who came to the sheep station once a week and took them to market. When the rabbits were breeding, they sometimes managed to capture 300 a day.

Even though Umberto enjoyed catching the rabbits, he was always seeking out new opportunities. He had heard through friends that he could make an excellent living by working in a sawmill at Swifts Creek near the New South Wales border. As Umberto asked around, others told him that the journey to Swifts Creek was 200 miles north-west of Melbourne and then a further 60 miles to Omeo, a small country town near the New South Wales border, before reaching Swifts Creek. He certainly had some thinking to do before making such a dramatic move.

With the rabbit catching Umberto was lucky if he earned £9 in a good week, not an excellent wage but enough to pay his rent. He thought if he moved to Swifts Creek and worked in the sawmill, he could earn up to £27 in an average week. Not being one to shy away from a challenge, it did not take long for Umberto to decide to move to an even more remote part of Australia for another chance at a better life.

Having never worked in a sawmill before did not phase Umberto. It turned out to be a great move as he learnt new skills, had a stable income, somewhere to live, good food and no concerns for his future. Time went by quickly, and he worked there until 1954 before feeling the need to move on again and do something different. In considering his next move, he was influenced by where his friends were going.

***

IN FOCUS: AUSTRALIA'S INTRODUCED RABBIT POPULATION

In modern Australia, rabbits are the number one pest due to the severe damage caused by the overgrazing of land and the threat to native burrowing animals. However, it was not always that way, with the rabbit industry having a profound effect on the lives of thousands of rural Australians.

There were no rabbits in Australia until European settlement in 1788 when five rabbits arrived with the First Fleet. Initially bred as a food source, an early settler brought in more hares and rabbits for hunting on his property in Victoria. In just six years the rabbits increased to an estimated 20,000 and within 20 years reached plague proportions.

In 1887, the Western Australian government built a 1,800-kilometre rabbit-proof fence, although this approach did not work because the rabbits jumped the fence, burrowed under it or bounded through when the gates were left open. Other methods tried in a futile attempt to control the rabbits included shooting, poisoning and digging up the maze of underground tunnels.

By 1910 rabbits had spread uncontrolled across Australia. In 1929 the rabbit industry was reported to be the largest employer of labour with some earning in a week up to ten times the rates of pay received by building and metal industry tradesmen. Even though rabbits were considered a menace, they were also a free source of meat during the Depression.

By far the most significant impetus to the commercialisation of the rabbit was the export trade in frozen rabbit carcases. Most trappers were from the ranks of the casual labour force that lived and worked in rural areas. During the 1930s and 1940s, some rabbit farmers earned £4,000 a year from rabbit skins. The trappers, who purchased the skins for market then earnt astronomical money during the 1940s and early 1950s with prices for carcases and skins pushing average earnings up to £50 a week.

By 1950, the rabbit population in Australia was estimated to be over 600 million. In 1951, the government released the myxoma virus into the wild rabbit population resulting in a rapid decline to about 100 million. Initially, mosquitoes were the critical transmitters of the disease, but they were unsuitable for the drier parts of Australia, so European and Spanish fleas were brought to Australia to spread the virus more widely. Some rabbits became resistant to the virus, and numbers started to increase again.

A Better Life

In 1952 some rabbit farmers were heavily dependent on the rabbit industry for the economic survival of their large homestead properties. After 1952, exporters sourced their rabbits from central Australia, which was an area too dry for the virus-carrying mosquito. By mid-1953 it was estimated that four-fifths of all rabbits in south-east Australia had died. Australian farmers continued to export frozen rabbit carcasses to overseas markets until the early 1970s.

CHAPTER 6

Cutting Sugar Cane

IN TALKING WITH FRIENDS, Umberto found three of his friends wanted to go to North Queensland for work in the cane fields. Umberto had no idea how far this was or how much work was involved but decided to go with them anyway. It was a big adventure for them all as they set off on their journey into the unknown. They travelled by train to Townsville on the north coast of Queensland, and then to Ingham, a small country town just north of Townsville. It was here where they were to about to work as they had never worked before.

During the early years of sugar cane production in Australia, the cane was cut manually. The cutting tool looked like a machete with a small hook on the end of it to catch and cut the sugar cane. There is no doubt this was backbreaking work as it also required lifting almost 14 tonnes of cane manually three times each day. It didn't take long before they realised they had to do this if they wanted to be earning the big money which had lured them there. They planned to be there for only the cane cutting season which ran from June to early December, finishing just after

Christmas, after which they would return to New South Wales. As it happened, each of them worked in Ingham for nine months until early 1955 before they moved elsewhere.

During this time Umberto wrote a letter to his older brother, Ercole, who was still living on the family farm in Italy. He asked Ercole if he wanted to come to Australia to live as there was money to be made if you worked hard. Ercole was happy to have received Umberto's message and didn't hesitate to accept, especially as Umberto had saved enough money to pay for his fare to Australia. Like Umberto, Ercole had to go through the same immigration processes as Umberto before boarding a ship for the long journey to Australia.

Shortly after he arrived in Australia, Ercole, Umberto and his friends Ascenzo, Mario and Pasquale started living together to save on living costs and to share each other's company. The cost of living in such a remote area was high, so sharing meant they were each able to save some money for things they wanted to buy. Because they worked harder than most others cutting cane, the wages they received were excellent and significantly more than what they had been earning previously catching rabbits or at the sawmill. Ercole also knew he had done the right thing moving to Australia as his salary was much more than he could ever have made on the family farm in Italy.

They lived in a small part of a massive shed on the farmer's property where they worked. They felt lucky and resourceful to get this accommodation as the farmer wasn't using the shed for anything, and no one else had thought to ask. The shed frame was made of rough-cut timber which

A Better Life

was hand-sawn from large trees from the property, with oversized barn doors and a corrugated iron roof. Some internal half-height walls provided a degree of privacy for bathing and changing clothes. The floor was cement, and although it was dry, it was dusty, cold and very uncomfortable to walk on after a long day cutting sugar cane. The living conditions were simple at best, although they did not mind.

They had old-style canvas stretchers for beds but no mattresses to provide comfort for their aching bodies as they tried to sleep through hot, steamy nights often while being bitten by mosquitos. There were also a couple of rough-cut wooden tables and a few old chairs in disrepair. It was at this table where they ate their meals and shared their stories. They would often talk for hours after dinner about what they eventually wanted to do and their dreams of a much better life than they had in Italy.

Cooking was always a challenge as they only had an old-style wood-burning stove, a few heavy cast iron pots and pans, and a kerosene fridge. The farmer provided them with a few of the bare necessities such as plates, bowls and cutlery which helped them out. It wasn't long before they found out that Mario knew how to cook and so he tended to do most of the cooking for all of them.

Each day Mario would finish work about one hour early to go home and prepare the evening meal. Cooking under these primitive conditions would have been a challenge for anyone, let alone someone who had already worked a full day cutting sugar cane. However, it was a system that worked for Mario as the others would wash the pots and dishes each day and clean up their living quarters.

No doubt cutting sugar cane by hand with a machete-like tool was never going to be easy. Those who did it found it to be incredibly hard manual labour, particularly more so in the sweltering heat of the North Queensland summers. Because they worked so physically hard, they had a big appetite and between them consumed half a cow each week and whatever vegetables they could buy. In today's terms, half a cow is around 100 kilograms of meat depending on the size of the cow, which they ate for lunch and supper. Mario was an excellent cook, so they were always satisfied.

Coming from farming families themselves, they were healthy young men, all putting in as much energy as they could. There were opportunities to make massive amounts of money for those who wanted to work harder than the others cutting cane, and it was commonplace for them to work until their hands bled. For these boys, while they all worked hard and suffered, they also earned big money for doing so.

In those days, before harvesting, the farming practice was to burn the sugar cane crops, although sometimes they could not because it rained. Burning the sugar cane crops always meant everything went black, often known as the 'black snow', as many families fondly called it. When the sugar cane crops burned, the air was thick with black ash which covered the workers from head to toe, leaving only the white of their eyes visible. One downside of the black snow was the race to get the washing off the line, and it was often a challenge to take it indoors before the ash came tumbling down. The alternative meant rewashing everything by hand as there were no washing machines that would reduce the workload.

Their work routine was the same each working day and never faltered. For five days a week, every week, they worked from 4.30am to 7.00pm. They were not allowed to work on weekends as the union was very strict and did not let that occur. However, if the men thought for a moment, they could get away with working on the weekends, they most certainly would have.

When their day started at 4.30am, they went to work with clean clothes, and by 11.00am they had to return home to shower and change, sometimes twice a day. After they ate their lunch and had a short rest, they went back to work until it was dark at 7.00pm. There were times there was so much work to do that they worked until 8.00pm to keep up. To work so hard in the sweltering heat of North Queensland was difficult at best and quickly sorted out those who could not deal with the weather or the pace of the work they were undertaking. These people left North Queensland to return to the colder climate of the southern states and set themselves up to live there instead.

During the sugar cane season after they cut the cane, one of the backbreaking tasks they had to do was to relocate a short temporary railway line twice a day. This railway line was used to hold the cane as it was harvested.

The railway line ran the length of the dirt track between the sugar cane rows and was laid out sideways. Umberto and his friends would load nine rows of burnt sugar cane bundles by hand either side of the railway line and then move 18 rows of the railway line for the next set of sugar cane bundles. There were six crossings, and the rails were six metres long, and they had to move the railway line across, sideways. The reason for loading the sugar cane in this way was because the width between the sugar cane crops was narrow, and they had to go sideways to harvest the cane.

In perspective, moving the railway line so that they could do their job meant they had to move more than 200 steel rails totalling 22 yards in length twice a day, each working day, Monday to Friday. They were all small men in stature but physically active and young. When Umberto was cutting cane, he weighed 136 pounds (62kg), and each section weighed about 209 pounds (95kg). He would often grunt and groan as he stood between the rails, picked them up in the middle part and balanced them carefully as he walked across 18 rail track girders that were 24 yards wide.

Umberto would often have to drag the rails across the railway line that was already down and stick the single iron pin into the double pin to rejoin it before they could use it. This manoeuvre required all of the other men to move quickly if they were to rejoin the rails or risk severing a foot in the process. While they knew that cutting sugar cane was physically demanding work, relocating the railway line was even harder. Umberto and Pascale would often do this task as the others were just not strong enough.

There is no doubt cutting sugar cane for a living was incredibly hard, backbreaking work. The sugar cane farmers had hundreds of acres of crops to be harvested by hand, and in the early days, there was no alternative. To add to this, the sugar cane farmers were under constant pressure and had to meet production requirements.

If they didn't meet production requirements, the government would try to limit their competition which would negatively impact after-sales income. After many months of doing this exhausting work, Umberto again began to think about his future and how he could do better. After all, he had come this far and wondered what else was in store for him on his journey through life in his adopted country.

***

IN FOCUS: THE SUGAR CANE INDUSTRY

In Australia's economy today, sugar is one of its most important industries worth around $1.75 billion annually. Interestingly, Queensland produces 95 per cent of the annual market, of which 85 per cent is sold on the world market. The sugar industry has become the cornerstone of many North Queensland communities, although it has not always been that way.

The First Fleet introduced sugar cane to Australia in 1788. In 1861, the first white settlers moved to North Queensland to grow sugar cane. Because the sugar cane flourished in the hot tropical weather, it wasn't long before the first viable sugar mill was established to process the sugar cane.

Until 1904, settlers used cheap convict workers, volunteers and illegal Islander labour to harvest crops. Migrants from Italy and other European countries began to arrive seeking work in the North Queensland cane fields. There were many Italian cane cutters, all of whom worked hard in harsh conditions with some earning enough to buy their own farms. The sugar cane crops were cut manually, picked up by hand and manually loaded into waiting trucks for transportation to the sugar mill. As farmers began to seek faster and cheaper ways of cutting and packing sugar cane crops, they eventually invented machines that could work anywhere, in any weather and under any conditions.

The sugar mills were typically located near the sugar cane farms, and during the cane season, they ran 24 hours a day, seven days a week. The milling of sugar cane is quite efficient with the fibre used as boiler fuel, the resulting ash and mud used as fertiliser, and the molasses used in distilleries or stock feed. The raw sugar is held in bulk lots with Australia having the most significant storage and handling system in the world.

There are significant benefits to the multicultural diversity enjoyed in many areas of Queensland, mostly due to the immigrants who contributed so much to the sugar industry. In North Queensland today, there are sugar cane farmers who are descendants of the first settlers and who celebrate their origins with annual events and festivals. In modern times there are some areas of Queensland where sugar mills have diversified, and sugar cane is used to develop ethanol, an alternative fuel for all sorts of vehicles.

CHAPTER 7

Farming Life at Millaroo

IN LATE 1954, UMBERTO'S attention turned towards the possibility of buying his own farm. A friend, also from Italy, made a proposition that was too good to refuse. He offered to sell him and his friend, Ascenzo, 600 acres in Ingham not far from where they were cutting sugar cane. It sounded remarkable, as his friend explained as 'new Australians' they could plant sugar cane. So, with little thought about the practicalities of such a purchase, Umberto and Ascenzo embraced the offer. Finally, Umberto's dream of a better life presented an opportunity to buy a farm — an incredibly attractive prospect. He felt he was doing what he wanted and building a better life for himself.

Umberto and Ascenzo were very excited and trusted their friend; after all, he was also Italian, so why wouldn't they? Without seeing the land, they paid £600 for the property in Ingham, which was incredibly cheap at the time at £1 per acre. Without knowing anything about the area, where it was and whether it was fertile, they not only bought the property, they also purchased an optional Chevrolet three-and-a-half tonne truck and a McCormick International tractor that their friend didn't want. They started making plans for their new farm, considered the crops they could plant and dreamt about how to manage the farm and make money as they had never known before.

Their excitement quickly faded when they realised the location of the farm was not exactly close to where they were currently cutting sugar cane. It turned out the farm was more than 180 miles south of where they were, in the town of Millaroo. Not only that, even though they dreamt of their own farm, they had no idea of what they were doing, or how it was going to work at a practical level. In spite of all the problems, they decided to take on the challenge and see where it would lead them.

In early 1955, they finished cutting sugar cane in Ingham and with no further thought about the challenges, made plans to move to Millaroo and start work on their sugar cane farm. However, they soon realised it was not going to be as easy as they first thought as there was no permit to plant sugar cane and initially and did not know they needed one.

These bureaucracy matters were not part of their dreams and not quite what they had hoped. However, they forged ahead and decided to try and get a permit. As quickly as Umberto applied for a permit, he received a rejection, without any explanation to understand why this had occurred. Not one to give up, in early January, Umberto and Ascenzo flew to Brisbane and met with representatives of the Sugar Cane Board to discuss their application for a permit to plant sugar cane in time for the next season.

Umberto was very confused about what happened next mainly because he felt he was given the runaround over the application for a permit. He had informally heard that their request had been refused due to the high amount of industry rules and regulations, which meant that production was not automatically increased each year but increased every decade or when it was required for the world markets. Not satisfied with the explanation he received, Umberto commenced his pushback with the government and was passed around from one department to another. After some time of being referred from one department to another, the Sugar Cane Board representatives said they understood his intention and then referred him to the Water Board to discuss his situation further. Umberto was quite frustrated when the Water Board told him to go to the Townsville branch to try and sort out the situation.

Umberto was prepared for more arguments with the Water Board in Brisbane and was not ready to give up. The Water Board offered them 60 acres of land a further 20 miles south of Millaroo as an alternative to the 600 acres Umberto and Ascenzo purchased. Again, neither Umberto nor Ascenzo appreciated where they were going to be buying. However, they decided to accept the offer and move on (and did not realise this was the same area as the 600 acres they had purchased). The proposal was a 99-year perpetual lease for which they paid 10 shillings per acre. To secure the property, they needed £1,500 in cash or assets available or to be able to take a loan for the money from the Agricultural Bank, a government-owned corporation that often helped farmers establish and manage their farms when it was economically viable to do so.

In getting together the deposit, they needed to sell the land in Ingham to raise enough money to buy the 60 acres of land offered by the Water Board. They were in for a surprise when they realised that even if the land in Ingham could be sold, they would not be able to raise enough money to buy the 60 acres. Luckily for them, they were able to obtain a receipt from the bank stating they had £1,500 so they could get the loan from the Agricultural Bank.

When they finally obtained the loan, it enabled them to build some small sheds to use for drying and storing tobacco after harvesting. Umberto felt he had no choice but to trust the bank manager if he wanted to have a prosperous future.

Umberto and Ascenzo were excited but still decided to push through and buy the second parcel of land without seeing it. The location of the property did not worry them. After all, it could not possibly be in a worse place than Ingham. After meeting with the Water Board and obtaining a loan from the Agricultural Bank, they were finally happy with their purchase. After so much frustration and the slow progress towards the purchase, they decided they should probably visit their new property at Millaroo. They started making their plans, and with the address in hand, they set out to make their way there.

As they looked for a taxi, they hailed the first one that passed by. After showing the driver the address of their new property, the driver was perplexed. After much frustration, Umberto and Ascenzo decided to go back to the Water Board to get more details about the actual location of the property. After some discussion, the Water Board told them where Millaroo was. Only then did they begin to wonder what they had done and what the future had in store for them.

To get to the land, they would need to take a flight to Townsville, a train to Ayr and then finally a bus to Clare. A journey of several days. So, they purchased the tickets on the next scheduled flight back to Townsville.

However, the flight was not without incident, and ten minutes out of Townsville, one of the engines turned off, and the plane suddenly descended around 6,500 feet. There were more than 40 passengers on board, and the resultant chaos saw one man, who had been in the toilet, fall out with his trousers down near his feet. The passengers all reacted in their own way with some laughing, some screaming and others crying as they thought they were going to die.

The pilot eventually regained control, and the flight tracked along the coast until arrival at Bowen where the aircraft could safely land on one engine. On arrival, they stayed and waited for a plane to come from Townsville before continuing their journey by train to Ayr.

It was Friday lunchtime by the time they arrived at the railway station, and they quickly jumped on the first train. As they did, they realised it was a livestock train carrying cattle and not a passenger train. However, they decided to stay on the train which stopped at every station along the way to make deliveries of bread and groceries and to let other trains pass. After a very long and tiresome journey, they arrived in Ayr some 20 hours later.

If that was not enough, what happened next really had them worried about where they were; although somehow they still managed to maintain their excitement about their big adventure. From Ayr, they travelled by bus to Clare, a small town in the Burdekin Shire where growing sugar cane was the main crop in the area. After finding the engineer from the Water Board, they went with him to see the land they bought at Millaroo. They were most surprised the road to Millaroo was bitumen. However, the surrounding area was all thick bush scrub with no one living there, as well as no infrastructure such as electricity or telephones. They quickly found out they were the first farmers in this area which meant a lot of work before the land would be suitable for growing crops.

Feeling somewhat deflated and tricked by the government into buying something that was not going to be profitable, Umberto and Ascenzo reassessed their situation. First, though, they travelled back to Clare, took the bus to Ayr, the train back to Townsville and then back to Ingham. It was a solemn trip as each of them felt they had wasted their money and time. However, it was not long before they picked themselves up and decided to make the best of a bad situation. Umberto being the eternal optimist, kept dreaming of a better life.

Umberto and Ascenzo knew they had some organising to do, and after some discussion with Mario and Ercole, they quickly put their plan in place. They retrieved the truck they had purchased in Ingham the year before and loaded their luggage into it, which they agreed that Ercole would drive to Townsville to buy supplies. As there was no housing at Millaroo, they decided they needed to buy a tent, stretcher beds, mattresses, kitchen utensils and grocery supplies, before making the slow two-day drive back to Millaroo to start their new life.

Now that they had a plan, this was an exciting time for them as they felt they were on a big adventure without knowing where it would lead. When Mario, Ercole, Ascenzo and Umberto arrived at Millaroo, they began looking around to where they might pitch their tent and set up their cooking facilities. They took their time as they had a lot of potential locations to choose from — amongst the trees, near the river, or in an area that had already been partially cleared.

It was late in the afternoon before they finally settled on an area that was towards the bottom of a hill and which appeared to have some protection from the elements.

"I think we'll set up the tents here. It looks like a good spot," said Umberto.

With darkness approaching and no means for lighting except a lantern they had brought with them, they worked together pitching the tent and setting up the stretcher beds and unpacking. Even though it was a sweltering hot afternoon, Mario set about collecting firewood from around the campsite and setting up the cooking facilities. He quickly prepared their evening meal so they could eat and settle in for the night. Exhausted from travelling, it was not long after they had eaten that the sun went down, and they quickly fell asleep.

It rained all through the night, and they were so exhausted that a thunderstorm that passed over them did not stop them from sleeping through until the next morning. Ercole woke up first and was a little panicked when he looked around the tent to see water flowing around his stretcher bed and all the way through the tent.

"Umberto wake up. Wake up", said Ercole.

Umberto woke up with a fright and snapped at Ercole saying "What has happened? What is all this water?"

"There's a foot of water flowing through the tent. We are going to drown," said Ercole.

"No, we're not. It's not deep enough," said Mario.

It wasn't long before Ascenzo woke up and couldn't understand what all the commotion was about until he too saw the water in the tent.

"Umberto, why did you pick a river bed?" said Ascenzo.

"Stop complaining. We didn't drown," said Umberto.

With that, Umberto stood up from his bed and paddled through the water until he made his way out of their tent. The rain had ruined all of their belongings. As he made his way outside, he saw there was water everywhere across the river bed. Ercole followed him outside although he did not like wading through the knee-deep water.

After watching some of their possessions float away, they decided they should find an alternative location for their campsite. They sensibly decided it would be better to go to higher ground where it was dry, away from their original campsite.

For the nights that followed, they relocated their tent away from the river to ensure they had no further issues when it rained. Over the next few weeks, they settled in and became accustomed to living in such a remote area.

They worked daily in the harsh conditions to clear the land of the thick bush scrub and trees. As the months went by, they struggled to make ends meet financially. However, there was little paid work in the area and indeed few job prospects in the future. The countryside was so rough, and the living conditions so harsh, that Mario and Ercole eventually decided to move to Melbourne temporarily in search of paid work.

Ercole lived and worked in Melbourne for four months before returning to Millaroo to continue working on the farm. Mario did not return to Millaroo and decided to settle in Melbourne where there was plenty of work available. Umberto and Ascenzo chose to stay at Millaroo even though neither of them had a license to drive the truck. They had some exciting times and mishaps in those first few days as they taught themselves to operate the truck in the thick bush scrub.

After a few weeks, they felt they had enough driving experience to get their driving licenses and so decided to drive the truck to the police station in Ayr. Even though it had been a hot night, they agreed they would both put their best clothes on to impress the policeman. To avoid the heat of the day, they travelled early in the morning and arrived at the police station well before it opened.

As they had nowhere else to go that early in the morning, they just waited in the truck until the police station opened. Being the first through the door at the police station is not always the best approach. However, they were keen to get their driving licenses and get back to the farm at Millaroo.

The policeman, already sweating from the heat, said: "What brings you two here today?"

They were both beaming with excitement as Umberto said, "We have come to get our driving licenses."

The policeman looked them both up and down and shook his head at their clothing, which were long shorts and a shirt with a collar. Their hair was combed neatly with a part to the side. He then glanced outside at their truck, which happened to be the only vehicle outside the police station.

With a loud, rough voice, the policeman said, "And how did you get here today? Who drove the truck that is out the front?"

Umberto and Ascenzo stood quietly with their heads lowered looking at the floor as they sheepishly answered together, "We drove here."

Umberto also said, "We were taking turns as our farm is more than 40 miles away."

The policeman went out to the back of the station and after a few minutes returned with some paperwork. After looking them over, reviewing the paperwork, and looking at them again, the policeman said, "Well, you both seem to be honest young men. I'll give you your driving licenses."

"Thank you, sir, this means a lot to us," said Umberto.

With the ink on their driving licenses still wet as they waved them in the air, they quickly walked out of the police station. They did not look behind them in case the policeman changed his mind, and they had to go back. When they got to their truck, they climbed in and sat relieved for a few moments while they thought about what had just happened.

A Better Life

"He does not even know if we can drive. He did not even check," said Ascenzo.

"Yes, let's not stop and question it. Let's just get going and get back to Millaroo," said Umberto.

They drove away slowly in the truck to avoid bringing attention to their departure; smiling, laughing and delighted they were able to get their brand-new driving licenses without much trouble. As they drove down the main street, they decided to stop at the grocery store to do some shopping for some general supplies before making the long drive back to Millaroo. After getting some essential items and groceries, they headed home. The arrived at Millaroo late in the afternoon and had time to sit and think about their day and how much of a difference having their licenses would make.

Over the next few months, Umberto and Ascenzo began to clear the land with a pick and shovel seriously. It was exhausting and backbreaking work to chop down the trees and dig out the roots with just an axe. However, they were somewhat creative in how they bought down the trees. They decided to make a winch to clear the trees by tying them to other trees and pulling the winch until the tree came down. Even though this was smart thinking, it was still backbreaking manual work in the searing, humid heat. Despite the conditions, they managed to down four trees a day. However, even with this progress, it was not long before they realised it was going to take years to clear the land before they could even think about planting any crops.

One day, someone from the local Water Board was driving by their properly when he suddenly stopped by the side of the road so he could see what they were doing. He climbed out of his car and walked over to where Umberto and Ascenzo were working.

"Hello, how are you going? It seems like you might need some help," said the man.

"Yes, it would be good, but we cannot afford to pay someone to help us," said Umberto.

"Well, I might be able to help. I know someone who has a bulldozer who could knock down the trees for a small cash amount. Are you interested?" said the man.

"Well, we have 20 acres. Can this person you know do that?" said Umberto.

"Yes, of course, I will make the arrangements," said the man.

Umberto found this man to be amiable, which was most fortunate for them. It was not long before the trees had been knocked down and it enabled them to remove the remaining dense scrub by burning the trees, while they continued to dig up the roots and prepare the ground for planting their crops. The process of clearing the land was a long and arduous process they had not anticipated; however, they were learning valuable lessons along the way.

***

IN FOCUS: MILLAROO

Millaroo is a small country town about 100 kilometres south-east of Townsville in the Shire of Burdekin in North Queensland, located close to the coastline and the Coral Sea.

A Better Life

The name Millaroo comes from Millaroo Creek, which was first recorded by surveyor Robert Abbott in 1895. Robert was a chainman (someone who works with a surveyor to measure distances) and later a surveyor with the South Australian Surveyor-General's Department between 1877 to 1881.

The town is predominantly a sugar cane growing area with underground water supplies to irrigate crops.

As at the 2011 census, 200 people were living in Millaroo, consisting of mostly older adults.

CHAPTER 8

Growing Tobacco

UMBERTO AND ASCENZO STILL still desperately wanted to grow sugar cane, although they found it challenging to obtain the necessary permits. They came to know of other farmers who had moved to North Queensland and in driving by their farms noticed the main crop was tobacco.

They had heard it was simple to plant and grew well in the hot conditions, so they decided to plant tobacco seedlings instead. They had already built a shed that could be used to dry and stack the tobacco and where it would also be prepared ready for auction. The shed had 10-foot verandas, and this was where they lived and slept, as well as where they cooked their meals.

The weeks went by, and by mid-1955, they were ready to plant for the following season. They felt they had learned enough to know that tobacco plants took about six months to grow. Then they had to harvest, dry and present their tobacco bundles to the auction. With their first crop, they expected to have a lower production rate although they had hoped the buyers would buy at least a portion of their tobacco. If they failed, Umberto knew they had to go back to cane cutting to make enough money to pay for the labour to cut and dry the tobacco and to pay the debts incurred during the tobacco season.

They decided to plant 11 acres of tobacco and 20 acres of cotton for their crops. They thought this was a good move as, at this time, there were no other farmers in Millaroo, or in the Burdekin Shire, who grew cotton crops. It was a significant risk as they did not know anything about tobacco or cotton. However, this was one risk they were prepared to take. It was trial and error as they worked their way through understanding how to grow a fickle crop such as cotton. However, their plants grew well, and they were very excited when in mid-December 1956, their very first crops were ready to be harvested.

There is probably no need to say that growing cotton was a whole new experience for them, and they did not have the knowledge to be successful, although a lack of education did not stop them. There was obviously no internet at the time, but they knew that cotton was ready to harvest when they could see that the cotton ball had blossomed and was white and fluffy. However, the trouble was they had no idea how to collect it. In a bold move, they decided to harvest the cotton themselves. After all, they felt it could not be that hard compared to cutting sugar cane.

In preparation for picking the cotton, they used old sacks with crudely made straps slung over their shoulder. To avoid the heat of the day, they started pulling cotton early in the morning but quickly learnt that picking cotton was not so easy after all. In plucking the mature fluffy cotton from the cotton bolls, they grabbed as much as they could in one hand before putting it in in their sacks.

However, this was a slow process because they were not wearing gloves and found it tricky to navigate the external parts of the cotton, which were incredibly prickly on their hands.

Struggling in the sweltering heat and bending over the cotton plants they kept on picking. Ascenzo's hands started to bleed, and he had had just about enough of picking when he said, "Umberto, this is not going to work for us. I do not see how we can continue to do this on our own."

Umberto did not want to give up as this meant failure, a concept with which he was not comfortable. He pretended not to hear Ascenzo as he did not respond immediately and kept working.

"I've heard about a bloke who has a cotton harvester in Rockhampton. I might give him a call to see if he can come and do this," said Umberto.

What a blessing that was. Ascenzo was very excited about the prospect of a mechanical cotton harvester that could pick the cotton. He was wondering just how long Umberto had known this as he said, "Can you see if he will come to Millaroo before Christmas to pick the cotton crops."

There was now no time to waste as the cotton had to be picked quickly before it spoiled. Umberto made some enquiries about the cotton harvester, and it was not long before he received word the man who owned the cotton harvester was prepared to come to Millaroo on Christmas Eve to pick the cotton crops.

They started to make plans and then adjusted the shed to store the cotton. Little did they know Mother Nature had a big surprise in store for them. They were about to experience the most challenging thing a farmer could experience potentially changing the course of their farming career.

Before long, Christmas Eve was upon them, and they were sitting under the shade of their shed.

"If we were back in Italy, it would be freezing," said Umberto.

"This searing heat is entirely different, and sometimes I wonder why we are here," said Ascenzo.

"You know, we are lucky to be here and owning our own farm," said Umberto.

With everything seeming to be under control, Ascenzo took the truck and left early in the morning to visit friends in Ingham. It was a long drive, and he had planned to stay only a few hours before returning to the farm quite late in the day. The man with the cotton harvester arrived and started harvesting the cotton. Umberto watched intently as the harvesting tractor made quick work of picking the cotton.

As Umberto prepared lunch, he had a feeling that the harvesting would not be finished by the end of the day. While this did not particularly worry him, he was concerned about when the harvester could return to finish the job so they could start grading and packing the cotton in the sheds.

It was around 3.00pm when Umberto and the cotton harvester were finishing off their lunch and resting. As a car pulled up near the shed, Umberto recognised the vehicle as the one the Catholic priest drove when on his regular visits to their farm and others in the area. Umberto's mood lifted as he and the priest chatted about the success of their first cotton crop and the size of the tobacco plants.

"You have done well with your farm," said the priest.

"Thank you. We are happy with the progress we've made, although it really hasn't been easy," said Umberto.

The priest nodded and said, "Yes, I understand that, before I go, I will give a blessing to the farm."

Umberto stood back as the priest walked around the garden near the shed and the edge of the tobacco crops. He blessed the farm and the plants and finished by saying a prayer, for which Umberto was grateful. Soon after, the priest got into his car and drove back to his parish. Umberto was very pleased and felt such a blessing could only go in their favour moving forward. The driver of the cotton harvester had now been at the farm for several hours picking cotton. He jumped out of the harvester and turned it off and walked back to Umberto.

"I am going to head off home to have Christmas with my family. I will be back in a couple of days to finish off," said the man.

"Please do come back quickly. We need to finish and start grading and packing the cotton. Thanks for what you have done so far," said Umberto.

With that, the man changed his clothes inside the shed and headed off in his old rusty car waving goodbye to spend Christmas with his family in Rockhampton.

By 3.15pm, Umberto was left on his own on the farm and started making plans for the coming days, forgetting the next day was Christmas Day. Fifteen minutes later, he noticed dark clouds beginning to form on the horizon. As he sat in the shade of the shed, he continued to watch the sky with anticipation as the clouds grew more substantial and quickly joined together creating what seemed to be a massive storm that covered the sky in darkness.

It was not long before the sky opened up, and a fierce hailstorm hit the farm. The cotton crop was stripped bare in just 10 minutes, and he could do nothing to save their precious crops. As Umberto looked around the farm, he saw the hail had destroyed the unharvested tobacco plants with nothing, but the bottom of the plants left. He just stood in disbelief, his head hung low, not knowing what to do.

A farmer puts their heart and soul into tendering their crops and losing it is one of the most devastating things that could happen to them.

Umberto was in a state of shock and did not know what to do. He drove out to the ocean headland to think about what just happened, and to work out how long it would take the farm to recover. As Umberto drove along the highway, the tobacco and cotton from his farm was floating away with the stormwater. By the time he got to the headland, he felt depressed. He sat in the car trying to work out how he was going to tell Ascenzo what had happened and after some time returned to the farm.

It was late afternoon by the time Ascenzo returned, and initially, he did not notice what had happened at the farm. He was in a good mood after spending the day with friends until he saw Umberto sitting on a chair at the front of the shed with his head in his hands.

"Why are you looking so sad?" said Ascenzo.

Umberto just looked at him, shook his head, and said, "Look around, what do you see?".

As Ascenzo looked around, he began to realise that something terrible had happened. He went into shock as the devastation around him started to sink in.

"The crops! What happened?" said Ascenzo.

Umberto was still clearly shaken and said, "A terrible hailstorm swept through. In 10 minutes, everything was gone."

"I just do not know how long it will take to recover from this disaster," said Umberto.

Ascenzo remained quiet with his head hung low.

Umberto was emotional as he said, "I will need to return to cutting sugar cane so we can afford to live and buy food."

"Umberto, I cannot cope with this. I am going to leave the farm. I just do not want to be here any longer," said Ascenzo.

Ascenzo was a broken man. However, Umberto was not prepared to give up. After much more discussion, they agreed that Ascenzo would leave the farm and that Umberto would buy out Ascenzo's share.

They had worked so hard to build the farm and for their business partnership to end like this was not what either of them had anticipated. However, Mother Nature had been cruel, and Ascenzo was no longer interested in farm life. He felt it was in his best interest to move on.

For their business partnership to be dissolved, there needed to be financial compensation which was a difficult thing to consider and agree. With no expectations, Ascenzo nominated a price for his half of the farm that would enable him to walk away. They decided that Umberto would pay half the cost of the farm, the difference being the income from the crops. Umberto was not able to pay Ascenzo straight away and had to leave the farm to cut cane and make enough money to pay him.

By the next season, Umberto had tobacco-growing again. Before long, the tobacco crops were mature enough to be harvested. After hiring enough labourers, the tobacco was harvested and hung to dry in the drying sheds before being prepared for the market.

However, it was a sad day again when Umberto sent his tobacco to market, but it did not sell. Still, he tried the next year again and went back to cutting sugar cane to repay his growing debts. Growing tobacco and not being able to sell it was a vicious circle and Umberto struggled to understand it when another opportunity arose.

It was 1959 when the Water Board offered ten blocks of uncleared land for anyone who wanted to apply to purchase it. Never one to pass up an opportunity, Umberto made an offer for one block and used his savings to pay for it. He spent some time trying to work out what to do with the thick bush scrub which covered nearly every inch of the property. This was until a local man with a bulldozer approached him and offered to clear the area. As the man had not mentioned a fee, Umberto assumed this would be at no cost. So, he agreed, and after the bulldozer operator had completed the job, he presented Umberto with a bill for £252, which Umberto could not pay at the time. He still did not know what to do with the land and offered it to the bulldozer operator as payment, but he refused.

A Better Life

Without giving it much further thought, Umberto continued to grow tobacco on his original farm and always had faith that he would be able to produce mature crops which would sell at auction. He continued to work hard, and for his next harvest, he had 12 tonnes of tobacco to offer at an auction, scheduled for the week before Christmas.

Leading up to Christmas, a potential buyer for his tobacco crop contacted him and travelled to his farm before the auction. Umberto was surprised when the buyer offered him £12,000 to buy his farm instead, subject to the purchase going through after the sale of his tobacco crops.

It was 22 December, and the auction was to be held in Brandon, close to Ayr, just beside the railway line. The sale was inside a massive shed in sweltering heat where over 100 tobacco growers and 20 customer representatives were all looking for the best deal, or so it seemed. There was much conjecture amongst the growers about who would sell the most tobacco for the best price. Umberto was quietly confident that he would do well. However, it was the buyers who ran the show and set the scene for the future of tobacco farming.

It was a hot and humid day as the tobacco farmers and buyers mingled amongst the bales of tobaccos. There were a lot of full bales of tobacco propped up around the shed, all for sale, not just samples which had been the case with previous auctions. As Umberto walked through the shed, he noticed the putrid stench from the dried tobacco was very strong in the sweltering heat of the day. The smell is something that always occurs with naturally dried tobacco. For Umberto and many of the tobacco farmers, it ended up being an awful day as it turned out the buyers did not want to buy tobacco from any of the tobacco growers that day.

The following Monday, Umberto decided to present his tobacco crop for sale at another local auction, close to his farm at Millaroo. As he prepared for the auction, little did he know he was about to find out the reality of growing tobacco was harsh and unforgiving. He decided to offer the whole 12 tonnes for sale at the auction. Each of his tobacco bales cost approximately £220. He made sure at least one bundle was standing up, a small opening made, and with the tobacco pulled out for presentation. The auctioneer for the buyers smelled it, looked at the leaves, and started to bid on it. Even though he was bitterly disappointed, he did manage to sell four tonnes of tobacco. However, the remaining eight tonnes were passed in at 36 pence a pound, although it should have been bought for 120 pence a pound.

In addition to the sale of his remaining tobacco crop falling through, the offer from the buyer who wanted to purchase his farm for £12,000 also fell through. Umberto could not even give away his bales of tobacco.

It took some time to find out why the tobacco was failing to sell at the time of these auctions. For some reason, buyers were not sourcing tobacco grown in the Burdekin area anymore. Umberto was extremely angry about this and did not understand why. He was also very stubborn, and rather than trying to give his tobacco away, he decided to burn the remaining eight tonnes to the ground.

Once again, Umberto was forced to cut cane to pay the bills and buy food for sustenance. His debts now totalled £4,000, but he still had to pay for everyday items, and always had the cost of growing more tobacco crops. With his next harvest, Umberto sold four tonnes of tobacco and recovered £3,000 but still had a £1,000 debt remaining with the Agricultural Bank. It was during 1961 that he continued to travel around cutting sugar cane in Ingham so he could save money and pay the remaining £1,000 and for the labour he employed to harvest crops, who were also his friends. Umberto began to feel there was no future in tobacco and made the difficult decision to stop.

During the 1962–63 sugar cane season, Umberto was away from the farm cutting sugar cane and working as a labourer in a local sugar mill to work hard to make enough money to pay his debts. Early one morning he was woken by the police banging on the door to present him with a summons.

"Mr Palombi, you have been served to attend court," shouted the policeman.

In shock, Umberto read the summons which was about the man who cleared his land in 1959 and who had presented him with a bill for £252. The court date was just two weeks away. So, it was not long before Umberto found himself in court to defend his actions in not paying the bill. There was no one acting on his behalf, so he decided to represent himself on this matter. Umberto knew he had not done anything wrong.

After waiting patiently in the docks, the judge called the next case, and Umberto presented himself and waited for what would become his fate.

"Mr Palombi, explain to the court why you did not pay the man, Mr Pasuli, who cleared your land in 1959?" said the judge.

Umberto was quite obstinate and forthright as he said, "Judge, I did not have the money to pay Mr Pasuli. I offered him the land as payment via a land transfer instead. He refused me at the time. There was nothing else I could do."

The judge turned his attention to Mr Pasuli and quite sternly said, "Is that right, Mr Pasuli? Did you reject the land which Mr Palombi offered?"

Mr Pasuli nodded and said, "Judge, I needed the money to buy food for my family, not the property."

The judge shook his head and said, "This case is dismissed. Mr Pasuli and Mr Palombi, this case should not have been brought into my court at all. Leave this court at once."

In August, after recovering from the court ordeal emotionally, Umberto was contacted by a real estate agent again about the sale of his farm at Millaroo.

The next day the agent travelled to Umberto's farm to make further enquiries about the possibility of selling the farm for Umberto. He pulled up just outside Umberto's house, and before Umberto had a chance to greet him, he jumped out of his car and said, "Umberto, how much do you want for your farm."

Despite being surprised, Umberto confidently said, "I want £5,000. I will not change my mind. That is what I want."

A Better Life

The real estate agent smiled and said, "I am happy to pay that," and immediately wrote him a cheque for a £500 deposit as a down payment.

Two weeks later, Umberto was happily preparing to leave the farm when he received some bad news. The real estate agents' lawyer called to advise that the sale of the land did not go through as the Lands Department had frozen everything. The lawyer asked if he could have more time to arrange for the deal. The delay gave Umberto time to think, and he decided to withdraw from the contract as he had decided he wanted to keep the farm.

A month later, the Lands Department announced they would be holding a meeting at the local hall in Millaroo with all the farmers in the region. When the day came, farmers including those who came from Clare and Dalbeg waited patiently in the hallway with anticipation — the government had never gone to the area before, let alone hold a meeting with the farmers.

There was much celebration amongst the farmers when the Lands Department cheerily announced they could all plant sugar cane, and those who grew tobacco, could now also grow sugar cane. The farmers who wanted to grow sugar cane still had to put in an application for the farm and to obtain a mortgage through the Agricultural Bank. However, Umberto's feeling of wanting to stay on the farm had turned out to be the best thing he could ever have done. Umberto smiled to himself and looked forward to a better life.

Karen Guest

***

IN FOCUS: THE AUSTRALIAN TOBACCO INDUSTRY

Tobacco growing in Australia started in 1818 and by 1850 farmers were cultivating tobacco in New South Wales, Victoria and Queensland. There were no concerns about tobacco's effects on health and so the industry blossomed over the next 50 years.

By 1936, the Federal Government fully supported the burgeoning tobacco industry and encouraged manufacturers to use a minimum amount of locally grown leaf to get a tariff concession on imports. There were still no real health concerns, and by 1945, research showed that three in four men and one in four women smoked regularly. However, over the next two decades, smoking rates fell as people died and others gave up due to health concerns.

Tobacco growing reached its peak in 1970 with 16,000 tonnes sold annually with most leaf purchased by local manufacturers before deregulation of the market. Working against the industry were significant social forces. From 1986 to 2006, the government placed bans on smoking in the workplace, along with bans on advertising in newspapers and magazines, broadcasting and point-of-sale. Graphic health warnings and plain cigarette packaging were also imposed on manufacturers.

During the 1980s, smoking declined rapidly due to many health issues. People became more aware of tobacco-related diseases, nicotine addiction, and the effects of chemical residues added during the manufacturing process. In the 1990s, the initial impact of the downturn in tobacco growing led to a decline in consumption. This was followed by the reduction in protective tariffs, which unfortunately led to illegal trade in tobacco (known as 'chop-chop'). The tobacco-industry reforms saw the government offer restructuring grants to assist farmers in leaving the tobacco industry and moving into other sectors. At the time, there were 600 tobacco farmers with most crops grown in North Queensland. By the end of 1995, there were 366 tobacco growers left, with 240 of those in Queensland.

In 2004 the last contracts for tobacco crops were issued in North Queensland with farmers voting for a Federal Government and industry-funded buyout of the industry. In 2017, commercial tobacco growing no longer occurred in Australia with most leaf used in Australian-made cigarettes coming from the US, Brazil, Zimbabwe and India.

Today, Australia's low smoking rate is the result of a sustained and comprehensive public policy effort from government and public health organisations. However, smoking still kills 15,000 Australians each year and costs $31.5 billion in health and economic costs.

CHAPTER 9

Sugar Cane Farming

UMBERTO WAS LOOKING FORWARD to being able to freely grow sugar cane crops without the threat of being banned. However, it was not long before he worked out the government was protecting their interests in allowing farmers to grow sugar cane in these areas, including Mareeba. By the end of the year, Umberto tried to apply for a permit. However, the government transferred block number 53, with £4,000 of debt to Umberto's brother, Ercole instead. Umberto decided to apply for another block, number 91, so he could also plant sugar cane crops. In April 1964, a permit was issued to Ercole to grow sugar cane, although Umberto did not receive one.

At this stage, Umberto and Ercole owned the sugar cane farm in equals shares, and Umberto needed to obtain Ercole's signature on the application to transfer half the ownership to him. This was not as simple as first thought as Umberto had to travel from Millaroo to Mareeba. In those days going anywhere was a big journey. Umberto rode a motorbike on this occasion, and it rained all the way. However, this was the only way that Umberto would be able to see Ercole and obtain his signature as he was happy to relinquish half the farm to Umberto at no cost.

At the time, the bank manager who previously gave Umberto money also happened to be in Mareeba. Umberto went to see him and arranged for a loan so he could provide Ercole with the funds to take on block number 53. Umberto was thinking more of Ercole than himself as he felt this was critical for happy family life. Umberto wanted to look after his brother, Ercole, who was married with children of his own. It did not matter to Umberto as he was by himself. Umberto felt this gesture was significant as there was no one else who would have done what he did for Ercole.

With a small amount of money in the bank, Umberto was still trying to survive and pay his bills and to buy food. However, it was not long before he went back to cutting sugar cane to make ends meet.

At this time, Umberto often worked with an Italian friend and would discuss different things or argue with him when they were annoyed with each other. Umberto was still trying to obtain a permit to grow sugar cane and not having much luck getting one, so he decided he would talk with his friend about how to deal with the government to obtain a permit.

"You know, I am very unlucky not to have a permit to grow sugar cane," said Umberto.

"Do you have any document to say you have a permit to grow tobacco?" said his friend.

"Yes, I do. Why are you asking me this?" said Umberto.

"Umberto, I suggest you get your documents together. Let us see what we can do," said his friend.

"Ok, then, give me some time to find the documents, and we can discuss again," said Umberto.

After reviewing the records, Umberto's friend suggested they go to Townsville to meet with the Queensland Minister for Agriculture. It was lucky for Umberto that the minister happened to be based in Townsville. Umberto's friend wanted to meet with the minister to see if he could do anything about granting a permit to grow sugar cane. It was a long shot. However, Umberto decided he did not have a lot to lose and set about planning to go to Townsville.

Upon arrival at the minister's office, Umberto was surprised by to see that the minster was wearing shorts, a singlet and work boots as if he had just come from a farm.

Umberto's friend had already prepared Umberto on what to say to the minister, and so sat quietly while Umberto did all the talking.

"Mr Palombi, please come into my office and take a seat," said the minister.

After they both took a seat, the minister said, "Please, talk to me about the permit issue that you have."

"Minister, these are all of the documents I have. You will see I have a permit to grow tobacco. I do not understand why I cannot also have a permit to grow sugar cane," said Umberto.

The minister looked at Umberto's records, moving them around, trying to see if there were something he could do that would help and give him the authority to grant a sugar cane permit. While he was doing this, Umberto was thinking a lot about the time he had wasted in the preceding 12 years and that he was about to lose everything. But he was at the point where he had nothing else to lose.

Umberto's frustration was beginning to show as the minister started tidying up the documents towards the end of the meeting.

As the minister handed Umberto his documents, he said, "Umberto, I have to go to Brisbane for the parliament sitting. I ask that you give me two weeks to make my decision. I promise you that I will see what I can do for you."

Umberto had no choice but to trust the minister and accept him at his word. Two weeks later, in mid-September, the minister invited Umberto back to his office to discuss his application for a sugar cane permit.

"Umberto, I promised you I would see what I could do," said the minister.

"Yes, Minister. I am happy to be invited back here to talk with you," said Umberto.

After a short silence, the minister said, "I am pleased to advise I can grant you a permit to plant sugar cane."

"Thank you, Minister. This means a lot to me."

It was a big surprise to Umberto that the minister was true to his word as no one had done that for him before.

They shook hands, and as Umberto left the minister's office, he felt a sense of pride that he had taken on the government and won. The government was not as bad as he thought, after all. Umberto was so pleased when he got back to the farm at Millaroo he quickly commenced planting sugar cane crops on his farm.

With the issue of the permit resolved, the bank could lend money to Umberto to develop his farm, and to buy the tractor and the machinery for harvesting the crops. Umberto

A Better Life

planned the first sugar cane harvest for 1965. Little did he know it, but growing sugar cane on his farm would have a significant impact on the rest of his life.

In those early days on the farm, and for around three years, Umberto lived under basic conditions as he struggled to grow his crops. Due to the farm's location, he had a rather unusual way of buying his weekly groceries. Umberto would write everything on notepaper and then on Mondays when the mailman arrived, gave him the list and some money to give to the grocery store. When the mailman was on the next run, usually by the Wednesday, he would deliver Umberto's groceries. There were times when Umberto would run out of food and had nothing to eat until the mailman came by again.

This way of life was just an existence; living in the bush with little contact with anyone and no way of quickly getting food. Living and farming in an isolated region, with few people to talk to and the nearest shops 50 kilometres away, was undoubtedly an incredibly tough life.

Sometimes he went for weeks without talking to anyone, although he did receive visits from salespeople trying to sell tractors and other machinery for the farm. However, he was building a better life and did not complain much. He just kept working hard and always moving forward.

Early in 1955 electricity became available in the area. However, the farm was not connected to the grid, which meant at night, there were only kerosene lamps for light.

There was a significant celebration when the electricity company finally connected the power to the house.

However, Umberto was soon at odds with the electricity providers as he was not always able to pay on time. The providers would then come to the farm and cut off the power. While this was difficult to deal with, Umberto just accepted it, paid his bills, had the electricity switched back on and moved on.

During that first year of growing sugar cane in 1965, Umberto planted 30 acres. He was strong and determined and at first harvested the crop by hand with a machete on his own. It took an extraordinarily long time — from May until December — to complete this massive task.

At the time Umberto decided not to hire anyone else to cut the sugar cane as he could do it himself. Due to the industry regulations, hired workers were only allowed to work five days a week, whereas Umberto could work seven days a week despite the searing heat and humid conditions.

Umberto had plenty of time to harvest the sugar cane and collecting 12 tonnes a day was not a big thing for him to do. To harvest 12 tonnes would take about four to five hours; the sugar cane would be cut and loaded onto the truck and then taken away to the sugar mill. This left time in the day for other farming, as well as the domestic duties he needed to do. He worked hard every day and was living his life the way he wanted. What could be better?

Quite suddenly and without any delays, Umberto had the influence to borrow money from the bank to further develop his farm. His life was once again changing quickly, although this time only for the better. He was able to start hiring people to drive trucks and transport his sugar cane crops from the railway siding to the sugar mill. Life was

A Better Life

indeed picking up for the better and Umberto continued to dream of a better life.

In 1966, Umberto bought a truck and entered into an agreement with his brother, Ercole, who had a front loader. Together they employed one man and between them manually harvested, loaded, and transported 6,000 tonnes of sugar cane to the railway siding (a small section of railroad track that opened onto the main track at one end) for transportation to the mill.

What they did was incredibly backbreaking work, but they were in their thirties and young enough to deal with it. Umberto thought he could do 20 hours a day but soon realised this was not possible. The type of work was very physical, and he felt that a person would not get depressed if they worked as hard as he did.

The months went by, and in 1968, technological advances saw the first full stick sugar cane harvester developed and made available to sugar cane farmers. The farmers had been waiting for this technology.

Umberto and ten other farmers in the same local area joined forces to purchase a harvester and other equipment including a loader, and a truck to transport the sugar cane to the siding. Umberto would subcontract to others and carried about 12,000 tonnes of sugar cane to the siding. All the while, he was still growing his sugar cane crops.

Umberto had a vision for tomorrow and prosperity. As he started to build his portfolio, first with his sugar cane farm, he also looked for alternative commercial opportunities. Around this time, there were some farmers troubled with depression who abandoned their farms. For many farmers, who were the pioneers of a fledgeling sugar cane industry, living in such remote areas was a challenging way to live. However, Umberto was strong emotionally and able to survive the toughest of times.

In September 1969, Umberto's 63-year-old mother, Maria, travelled from Italy to Australia to see for herself what it was really like in this far away land. Umberto's father, who was still alive at the time, chose not to travel as he had no interest in visiting a place that was on the other side of the world. Maria also wanted to meet Ercole's family, and to see what Umberto was doing in a foreign land.

As Umberto's mother spent time with them, she found there was a significant difference between Ercole and Umberto, mainly because Ercole had a wife and four children. However, she was happy when Umberto confessed, he had been planning for three years to return to Italy for a visit, although there was always a reason why he could not go. However, there was a change in the air and the only one who did not know it was Umberto.

CHAPTER 10

Family

TIME WAS PASSING QUICKLY for Umberto. He was getting older and thinking about settling down. He had now reached a stage in his life where he was thinking about what the future might bring for him in terms of marriage and a family.

By the end of December 1969, after many painful years of growing tobacco and sugar cane, and reluctantly accepting he sometimes failed to reach his goals, he still considered himself to be a pretty good catch for any young woman looking for a husband.

Umberto's mother was due to return to Italy, and impulsively, he decided to go with her for a well-deserved, three-month holiday. After quickly packing a small suitcase he travelled to Italy leaving his new life behind, but just temporarily, as he was determined to return to Australia. His vacation turned into an unexpected adventure, and it was more of a surprise to him than anyone else that he ended up staying for 15 months.

He spent several months meeting and going out with numerous women trying to decide if one could be his wife and return to Australia with him. It was such a fantastic time of his life, and while things continued to change quickly, he kept true to his dreams of a better life.

In April 1970 Umberto was visiting with his younger brother Ezio and his wife, Iliana, for a short period. It was during this visit that Umberto first heard through his sister-in-law about a young woman called Victoria. As soon as Iliana spoke about Victoria, without meeting her and almost immediately, Umberto felt a connection and just knew she was the one who would become his wife.

Victoria had been in the convent since she was 17 years old and had been training to be a nun for ten years. After talking at length with his family, Umberto obtained the address of the convent in Rome, located close to the Colosseum, where Victoria was living. Each week, over several weeks, Umberto visited Victoria at the convent, although their visits were nearly always short and never in private. It took some time, but Umberto, with the help of Iliana, eventually obtained approval from the convent for Victoria to transfer to another convent in Latina.

The Latina convent was five miles from where he was staying and much more convenient for visits. Umberto felt he was incredibly lucky that Iliana was able to help in arranging for Victoria's transfer, which made it very easy for him to see her. Umberto and Victoria continued to meet, although this was still in the gardens of the convent.

The day came when Umberto decided they needed to take the next step in their relationship. As they were sitting quietly in the convent gardens, Umberto asked Victoria to go with him for a holiday away from the convent. Victoria agreed, and Umberto said to her that it may take some time but that he would make the arrangements.

It was August 1970, when arrangements were made for Victoria to travel to Sezze for a two-week vacation. It was during this time they made firms plans for Victoria to leave the church, marry Umberto and travel to the other side of the world. Once Victoria left the church, there would be no returning at any time.

With the decision made, Umberto and Victoria quickly married at a small ceremony in the local church. They decided to live in Sezze for several months to get to know each other more, and less than a year later in September, their first child, a boy, was born.

They stayed in Italy for another couple of months to allow Victoria to properly recover from giving birth. Everything went well, and Victoria recovered quickly, and it was not long before they were all ready to travel. In April 1971 Umberto and his new family moved to Australia and the next stage of their big adventure.

✱✱✱

IN FOCUS: WOMEN WHO BECOME NUNS

Across the world, in any number of religious orders, some women choose to become nuns and take a vow of poverty, chastity and obedience. In doing so, they leave mainstream society behind to live a life of prayer and meditation within the confines of a convent.

In Italy, a predominantly Catholic country, the process of becoming a Catholic nun is long and slow. Young women who are candidates to become a nun go through a process of praying, meeting other sisters, talking with a mentor, contacting a religious community, working with the vocation director and joining their chosen community.

A woman who wants to become a nun must take their final vows and make an ultimate commitment and must not change their mind or break the three original vows — poverty, chastity and obedience.

The vow of poverty means a nun must work for, and give their income, to the convent. The vow of chastity means all types of romantic or sexual relations are forbidden, and they are not allowed to marry or have sex, enabling them to focus on their vocation and service to God. The vow of obedience means a nun must obey their convent mother superior in day-to-day tasks and other duties on behalf of the convent, as well as the rules of the church and God.

In 2016, Italy's Catholic community accounted for 80 per cent of its population of 62 million. Even so, with fewer women becoming nuns each year, there is a concern the number of sisters is reducing so rapidly there may be none left by 2050. These figures are consistent with the worldwide decline in numbers of women becoming nuns. In Europe alone, the number of women becoming nuns dropped from 400,000 in 1997 to less than 300,000 in 2015 and continues to fall by approximately 8,000 each year.

CHAPTER 11

Losing Bruno

WHEN UMBERTO, VICTORIA AND and their infant son arrived at Millaroo, they did not have a proper house to live in or a place to call home. For a long time, they lived in the machinery shed on the farm. While they lived in the shed, Umberto set about building their family home, which was finished by the end of November 1972. After their second child was born, they moved into their new family home. Their life went on as well as could be expected as they raised their children and worked on the farm.

From all perspectives, they had a good life and were happy together living a life that others only dreamed about. In August 1974, their third child, Bruno, was born by caesarian section with no difficulties. While Victoria and Bruno were still in the hospital, Umberto was visiting with them. During the visit, the nursing sister took Bruno to where the other babies were in the nursery, and as she did, she commented that she thought there was something wrong with one finger on Bruno's hand. Umberto had noticed this too, although he thought nothing more of it at the time.

Life went on, Umberto and Victoria lived peacefully with their children and enjoyed their life on the farm.

However, a minor incident would soon cause their life, as they knew it, to change forever. On an ordinary day on the farm in August 1978, when Bruno was just four years old, he grabbed a sugar cane leaf with his tiny hand, and it scratched him on the first joint of his finger.

Although the scratch did not appear to be too thick, after a couple of weeks it was not healing so they decided to take Bruno to the doctor who said it was just a scratch and not to be worried. A couple of months went by, and the scratch still had not healed, so they returned to the doctor for a review. The doctor was still not concerned and advised them to return home.

The small, innocuous scratch slowly improved over ten months and was eventually forgotten. In April of the following year, Umberto and Victoria travelled to Melbourne during the school holidays returning at the end of April in time for school on a Monday morning.

It was a Saturday night when Bruno complained about feeling sick, and early in the morning, around 2.00am, they decided to take him to the doctor. However, Bruno, who was talking like an old man, and said that it was ok, and they could go in the morning.

The next few days were a blur as they drove back and forth around 55 kilometres each way to the doctor in Townsville. On Monday, the doctor had given Bruno some medicine, but by midday, on Tuesday, he seemed worse, so they returned. As soon as the nurse saw Bruno, she immediately realised he was very ill. Unfortunately, the doctor was on his way home. She managed to locate him and pleaded with him to return quickly to the surgery to review Bruno.

After returning and examining the child, the doctor diagnosed him with pneumonia and admitted him to the Townsville hospital to receive intravenous medication. Bruno was admitted to intensive care and treated by three specialist doctors during the night.

With Bruno under the care of the doctors at the hospital, Umberto decided to return to Millaroo. The night was long, and early the next morning, he returned to Townsville, not knowing he was too late. Bruno had passed away in the arms of his mother on 4 May 1979 due to complications from a tetanus infection.

Even though Bruno had passed away, Umberto was able to visit him to say goodbye. He held Bruno close to his chest and felt the warmth that was still in his little body. As Umberto held him close, he noticed Bruno's finger was black where the scratch had been. Umberto remembered when Bruno had been born, his finger was scarred, and therefore he felt perhaps it was his destiny to pass away young. A few days later, in an incredibly moving service, young Bruno was laid to rest in the family crypt just outside of Ayr.

Umberto and Victoria tried to move on with their lives, although life on the farm was not the same without Bruno. While they still had to care for their other children, the death of Bruno was all-consuming.

The first seven years following Bruno's death were extremely difficult for them both. Each day that passed, they did their chores and whatever else they had to do to get through the day. However, Umberto and Victoria suffered much during this difficult time and in silence. Looking back, Umberto regretted that he and Victoria did not speak of Bruno to each other or to other people. Umberto felt this had to be the worst time in his entire life as it is for any parent who loses a child, no matter what the cause.

Both Umberto and Victoria suffered in silence for many years, although Umberto thought Victoria had worked through the emotions before he did as she appeared to be coping a lot better. He had thought this because she had supported him for many years, and he, therefore, believed she was doing much better than he was. It was sometime later after Umberto's grief had eased that he was able to see that Victoria had never fully recovered from losing Bruno.

For Umberto though, and during the darkest of times, he felt Bruno's spirit was present with him always. He thought that Bruno would often come back and talk to him about getting on with his life. The first time he had this experience, and from that moment onwards, he felt that Bruno was helping him to move forward with his life and so accepted that he had passed away. To this day, Umberto believes that Bruno is still with him, pushing him to move forward. Even now, Umberto says he still remembers every minute of playing with Bruno all those years ago.

It was not until 1991 before Umberto felt he was able to move on with his life. As soon as he felt ready and to help himself get stronger emotionally, he made an unprecedented move into property development and constructing his first block of five residential units in Ayr. Umberto knew nothing about property development;

A Better Life

however, he was willing to try it and as always, make a better life.

In 1993, Umberto planned a visit to Italy with Victoria. However, there were issues in obtaining her passport. When the time for departure was just a week away, he was lucky the Ayr postmaster did his best to get her passport from Brisbane by having it forwarded by express mail. However, time was short as they were supposed to leave the following week.

In the end, Umberto decided he would go to Canada first, although Victoria chose not to travel with him. Umberto spent ten days in Canada to visit with his uncle whom he had not seen for more than 50 years.

Umberto and Victoria had supported each other through the worst time of their lives. However, while they had tried to help each other at every move, Umberto and Victoria decided they could not continue together, and while Umberto was in Canada, they decided to separate. During his time in Canada, Victoria telephoned to say the residential units he had built in Ayr had sold quickly and that he had to return soon to finalise the sale.

Shortly after Umberto returned from Canada, Victoria decided she no longer wanted to live on the farm and left. It was a struggle for Umberto, but he stayed on the farm on his own for another six years continuing to grow sugar cane until 1999. Eventually, he realised that something needed to change, and he and Victoria divorced.

Karen Guest

***

IN FOCUS: THE WRATH OF TETANUS

Tetanus is a severe disease that causes painful muscle contractions, particularly in the neck and jaw, and affects the nerves in the brain and spinal cord. It is sometimes referred to as 'lockjaw' because it typically causes jaw spasms. It is not a contagious disease but is often fatal.

It is caused by infection with a bacterium, Clostridium tetani, which produces a toxin that attacks the nervous system. Symptoms usually take up to 21 days to show.

The bacterium lives in soil, dust and manure, but can be found anywhere. A person can become infected if the bacterium enters the bloodstream through an open wound, even a small prick from a rose thorn can become infected. Some injuries are more likely to become infected, including compound fractures, deep wounds, wounds containing wood splinters and any contaminated wound.

The tetanus vaccine was first introduced in 1939 to vaccinate the armed forces personnel. In the 1940s, a diphtheria and pertussis vaccination program became available for infant children. By 1953, a diphtheria-tetanus-pertussis three-dose vaccine was introduced. In 1975, the first national vaccination schedule recommended and funded the three-dose vaccines for children, a booster combined diphtheria-tetanus vaccine approved and supported for five- to six-year-old children, with a booster dose every five years.

In Australia now, few people contract tetanus due to immunisation with the government hosting The Immunise

Australia Program that funds the purchase of vaccinations to protect millions of Australians from preventable diseases, including tetanus.

CHAPTER 12

Building a Portfolio

IT WAS A TOUGH decision, but Umberto eventually walked away from sugar cane farming. He had quickly established a reputation as a property developer in the blossoming building industry in Townsville. It was during 1992, while he was still with Victoria and living on the farm that he spent a significant amount of time travelling between their farm at Millaroo and initially Ayr, and then to Townsville to do whatever needed to be done to complete his building projects. In doing this, Umberto did things that other people could not or would not want to do. However, he was enthusiastic about embarking on this adventure.

At first, he found it was not easy to develop his knowledge and reputation in property development. Along the way, he had a lot of opposition from people who would not help him, who discriminated against him, and who gave him bad advice. Not one to ever give up, he forged ahead with his plans to build property and to make a better life for himself and his family.

His transition from a sugar cane farmer to a property developer was due in part to a friendship he developed with a real estate agent who introduced him to a local builder. The transition was relatively simple, and after a few conversations, he started his first project — a block of five residential units in Ayr.

Building residential units in a regional town would not be a natural process for anyone, let alone for someone for whom English is not their first language. To navigate the local council building requirements was a challenge, and what he could not learn or know, relied on others to help him. For the most part, he financed the project and subcontracted to others to do the building works. During the development stage, he engaged an architect in developing the building design, tendered for the works and then hired a builder to build the property. Subcontracting to others worked quite well, and he was delighted with the outcome.

He learnt a lot from this first project, although he did not construct the properties himself as he did not have the skill set. From this first experience, he made a reasonable profit and reinvested the profits into other projects so he could keep expanding his building portfolio.

Umberto was so pleased with this builder's work for the next three years he used that builder and made a good profit with every property. He was not sure about what he was doing and along the way, took some significant risks and found out how to do things through research and experience.

His builder did all the discussions with the local council and took control of the building process. The same builder introduced him to the bank manager, who was financing his investment properties. There was a reasonable degree of trust between Umberto, the builder, and the bank manager, although he made sure he had written contracts with the builder to do the work.

After a few years, Umberto found that establishing his building portfolio was not that difficult after all. He was in a sound financial position, and although he had little cash, he was asset rich. Umberto always believed he would do well and had no thoughts of failure. As the market was booming, he did not expect to lose money. For Umberto, the risks taken turned out to be excellent business decisions. Despite criticism from his friends he decided to do it anyway.

Once he understood how to do things, and felt the success from his property investments, he felt there was nothing that could stop him from continuing to build his portfolio. Umberto had never anticipated being a property developer, although he was never one to shy away from hard work. What he did during the next five years would undoubtedly be difficult for most people to comprehend.

Umberto continued to push himself and concentrated on his dreams. During the same year as the first block of units were constructed, he built another block of four units in Townsville, another five units in Ayr in 1993, and a further five units in Townsville in 1994. He was doing well, but things were about to change.

After he constructed another five units in 1995, the market dropped, and he could not sell or rent any of the empty units. When he felt the market was picking up in 1997, he decided to build another four-unit complex by continuing to go back and forth between his farm and Townsville. During this time, he was fortunate to be able to secure suitable tenants for his properties. He had been building for five years which was long enough now to know that he wanted to continue.

It got to the point there was no reason for him to continue working on his sugar cane farm at Millaroo as there was nothing there and no prospects. His son was not interested in staying on the farm and had bought a semi-trailer transporting freight across Australia. In 1999, it was a tough decision for Umberto when he sold his sugar cane farm. As he bounced back, he made a bold decision to enter the commercial property market.

An unexpected opportunity arose that allowed him to purchase a small shopping centre in Townsville before any large shopping centres had opened. As part of this venture, he had a lot of success with an internet café. The opportunity came about due to the sale of his original farm which had been for sale since the 1950s. During the mid-1970s, he held an auction with 30 potential buyers, and when there were no offers, it remained for sale. During 1999, in an unexpected twist of fate, a real estate agent met with Umberto to see if he was interested in swapping his sugar cane farm for the shopping centre in Townsville. This was a decision he did not take lightly although he saw it as an opportunity and did the deal for the shopping centre.

At the time, there were only four tenants which included a chemist, a general store, an office, and Kentucky Fried Chicken. In 2000, he opened a computer games shop, which had just a few computers initially, although this quickly grew to 32 units. The computer games shop was booming, so Umberto employed a manager who leased the shop from

A Better Life

him for the next ten years. The manager was a Sri Lankan immigrant and having some empathy for him as a migrant, Umberto also gave him a small amount of money to help him improve the business.

It was during 2002 that the property market picked up again, and so Umberto sold the last of the residential units from the ones he constructed in 1995. He was fortunate enough to be able to construct another eight units in 2003 and sold those in 2006, again for a reasonable profit. Never one to give up he also built another four-unit residential property in Townsville, where he lives today, and extended the shopping centre complex.

The computer games' shop manager travelled to Winnipeg, America, to buy the technology for the computers to control them. When the internet café first opened, there was an issue in that there was no record of when someone started or finished. The manager researched a technical solution available in Canada, which resulted in each desktop computer having a new technology installed for a $30 license. This meant every time someone was using a desktop computer, and it ran out of time, users would need to pay for more time to keep the game or the internet going.

By this time, Umberto had 54 computers and decided to build new office space specifically for them, moving into the new facility by the end of 2006. By 2010, due to the increase in home computers, the business deteriorated quickly causing the manager to close the store and give it back to Umberto.

At the time of writing Umberto's story, he still had ownership of the shopping centre which is leased to six tenants, including a chemist, dry cleaner, sushi café, technical college, natural herb grocery store, office space and a computer store. In total, he has 946m2 on 2,000m2 of available land that is entirely tenanted. He firmly believes in today's market, he is incredibly lucky to have a full tenancy, particularly so, considering Townsville has 60 per cent of similar commercial property types empty.

Many years earlier, when Umberto burnt his tobacco crop, many people considered it an error in judgement. It turns out he had the last laugh as other tobacco farmers carried on for another three years with debts three times higher than he did. He experienced the same aggression when in 1999 when he swapped his sugar cane farm for the shopping complex. When the market turned around, the farmers went bankrupt, but not Umberto.

CHAPTER 13

Friendships

HAVING A REAL FRIENDSHIP with someone means there is no judgment or jealousy; there is a level of trust they will be there for you when you need them, and there is mutual respect. A person might be fortunate to meet someone like this once, a person who touches their lives in a way they have not experienced before. If you are lucky, that friendship will last a lifetime. Umberto had few real friends like this. Even though he found it easy to talk to people, making friends was something he did not do easily. Far from his native Italy and on the other side of the world, he met a family who touched his heart, and their friendship spanned decades.

In 1961, Umberto met Michelangelo (Mick) Ragonese when they worked together for a time cutting sugar cane. When Umberto stopped tobacco farming, and after cutting cane with Mick for a short period, they travelled to Mareeba in North Queensland. They had decided to spend time with Mick's brother, Giuseppe (Joe) who was share farming tobacco crops in the area. Share farming was widespread and was when a farmer leased land and gave a percentage of their crops to the landowner. This ideology provided an opportunity for some farmers to build their experience through sharing the property with others, without the financial risk often taken by the owner of a farm.

Mick and Umberto worked tirelessly for Joe and helped him to prepare his fields to get ready for planting tobacco in time for the next season. Umberto thought that Joe did not need the help, but both Mick and Umberto needed the work and so accepted Joe's offer. It did not matter what type of work had to be done; they were happy to do it and fortunate that Joe went out of his way to help them.

The work was hard manual labour and included clearing the trees and preparing the soil. However, the bush was dense scrub and challenging to cut down and remove. To speed things up, Joe hired a bulldozer, and in no time the bush has been cut down. Mick and Umberto set about picking up the branches and leftover roots, although it still took time to clear the land. It would have been incredibly hard work doing this under any conditions, let alone in the hot and humid conditions of North Queensland.

Both Mick and Umberto stayed with Joe and his wife, Agata, on the farm while they did this work. At the time, they had two young children, Frances and Elena, who spent their days running around the farm. Eventually, Mick and Umberto left and went on their way, continuing to look for more work. Sometime later, Umberto found his way to Home Hill in Townsville cutting cane, before moving to Ingham to do the same thing. He then went to Giru located about halfway between Townsville and Ayr on the main highway that joined the two towns.

The three of them remained close friends, even though they were living in different locations. Umberto and Joe stayed close friends although it was some ten years later in 1974 when they met again in Innisfail for St Alfio. For the Italian people, St Alfio is a religious and cultural festival, otherwise known as the 'feast of the three saints' which brings people together in celebration of their faith. They had a great time together, catching up on what each other had been doing in the preceding years.

Time passed by, and they caught up again when Umberto travelled to Mareeba to visit with Joe and Agata for a holiday. Joe and Agata now had two other children, Anna and Franco. Franco was the same age as Umberto's son and Bruno was still in nappies. One day, Agata took time out of her own busy day to take Umberto and his family to the Atherton Tablelands near Mareeba. Umberto recalls he had a lovely time on that trip, and will never forget the unconditional kindness shown to his family.

Over the years Umberto and Mick also remained friends, although after Mick married his beloved Maria, they settled in Ayr, west of Townsville. As Mick was now settled and planning to work in Ayr to support his family, he decided to cut sugar cane for a living on the surrounding farms. It was not long before they had a son, Frank, and shortly after a daughter, Frances. It was an incredibly happy time when Mick asked Umberto to become Frances' godfather. Over the years they remained close friends, and even though they were somewhat separated by distance, they often travelled to visit each other during the holidays.

In 1979, Joe and his family moved to Brisbane in search of a better life and to raise their children. They would often return to Ayr for holidays to see Mick, and always made time to visit with Umberto at his farm in Millaroo. While they never stayed over with Umberto, they would visit for the day and stay until the early evening. During the day, they would relax and catch up, have a barbeque and enjoy each other's company before returning to Ayr. Such was their friendship, they could do that, even if it were just for a short time, and they remained friends for decades.

Umberto considered both Mick and Joe to be his compare and were close friends even though they were separated by distance, with Mick in Ayr and Joe in Brisbane. A bond with a compare is something hard to explain to non-Italians. It is a very dear and special relationship, one that is hard to break.

Umberto is unable to explain why he and Joe remained friends, except to say they had mutual respect and understanding of each other. They had both been through a lot in their childhood and then migrated to Australia; they felt a strong bond that nothing could separate. Umberto felt there was something between them the day they met, and suddenly when he cleared land for Joe, he felt something unexplainable. Umberto believes that when you meet someone for the first time, you either like or dislike them. Joe was one of these men who he loved and felt a strong bond with that stood the test of time.

Over the years, Umberto has never met anyone else like Mick and Joe. Others knew them and knew that Umberto was friendly with them, but they did not have the same relationship. Umberto feels a person can have many friends, but the respect for someone regarded as a compare does not change but instead gets stronger. It is often easy to distinguish between a friend who would do anything for you, from another who is just a friend but who would not go out of their way to help you. Joe was one of those people who would go out of his way to help others no matter what.

Umberto always thought about Mick and Joe and how close they were as if they were a part of his family. As time passes, people grow older and wiser, friendships come and go, relationships can change, but a real friendship will always remain. Umberto credits Mick and his family with the relationship they had and the bond he had with Joe and his family. Their friendship withstood the challenges of time and separation, and he always remembered what they meant to each other. However, life goes on and changes when it is least expected.

In August 2011, when Umberto heard Joe was ill, he dropped everything to travel from Townsville to Brisbane to be with his friend. He was grateful to have been able to spend some time with him and his family. Sadly, Joe passed away the night Umberto arrived. Then in 2016, Mick unexpectedly passed away in the aged care home where he resided with his wife, Maria, who also passed away shortly after.

Life goes on for Umberto, albeit in a different way without the friendship of Mick and Joe. However, what is in the heart remains in the centre and in the memories of those who are left behind.

CHAPTER 14

Second Chances

SOMETIMES PEOPLE ARE LUCKY and given a second chance at life. It was 2002 when Umberto was 69 years' young and met the love of his life, Anna. Anna is also Italian but has spent most of her adult life in Alberta, Canada. She migrated to Canada as a young adult and married early; raising three sons in Grand Cash, a remote area in Alberta and later divorced her husband.

Umberto and Anna believe how they met and fell in love was fate. There are many stories about people who live near or know the same people, yet they might never meet and may never know how close they came to be able to change their destiny. For Umberto and Anna, little did they know how close they were through their relatives and other people they both knew. Two of Umberto's relatives, Uncle Oldirico and Aunty Ida, had migrated to Calgary, Canada and they happened to know Anna. When Anna first arrived in Canada in 1959, she worked with Oldirico and Ida, so they go back a long way.

When Umberto travelled to Canada in 1993, he met Antonia (Tony) and Angela through some friends, and they developed a friendship of their own. Unbeknown to Umberto, Tony and Angela were friends with Anna, and she often went on holidays with them. In early 2002, Anna decided to accompany Tony and Angela on holidays to Australia to visit Angela's brother in Sydney. As part of their holidays, Angela and Tony chose to visit Umberto in Townsville and asked if they could bring a friend, Anna, before returning to Canada. Umberto was happy for them to bring their friend with them and looked forward to their visit.

While in Townsville, Tony, Angela and Anna wanted to go to South Mole Island, 300 kilometres south of Townsville, for a few days. Umberto agreed to join them, and they had a great time walking around and enjoying the scenery of the Whitsunday Islands. Following this, they travelled to Cairns and the Great Barrier Reef before returning to Townsville.

During this time, Umberto and Anna quickly developed a close friendship and realised they wanted to be together. It was a whirlwind romance which took them both by surprise, especially at their age. However, they did not care what others thought, and Umberto agreed to go to Canada, although at the time they made no firm plans as to when this would happen.

In April 2002, and after many long-distance telephone calls, Umberto travelled to Canada to see Anna and to spend time with her and her family getting to know each other further. Anna's family had pre-booked their family holiday on an Alaskan cruise in June. However, now that Anna had met Umberto, she insisted he go with them. After some quick thinking and telephone calls to the cruise line, Umberto went on the cruise with Anna and her family and had the most fantastic time. Following the cruise, Anna decided to return to Townsville with Umberto. It was the start of their new life together, and they made plans for their future. Initially, they thought they would have five years together before one of them passed away. During the early days, Umberto spent most of his time in Australia, returning to Canada with Anna when she wanted to be with her family (and to avoid the heat of North Queensland).

In Canada in December 2002, Umberto and Anna married on Umberto's 70th birthday, with much love and support from Anna's family. More than 60 people attended their wedding, including four of Umberto's relatives, and Umberto's daughter and her husband; and their mutual friends, Tony and Angela. Umberto and Anna did not want any gifts; however, they did say they would be happy to receive a gift for a children's charity. They received many donations for this charity with a range of clothing for babies through to eight-year-old children. This was a special time in their lives which they shared with their family and friends.

Umberto and Anna were happy together, although at times it was a struggle due to their age. Umberto says they married because Anna wanted to be married, although he did not mind either way, as he is the type of person that once he commits he will follow it through, no matter what. Some would say this is no different to every other decision Umberto has made in his life. It does not matter to him what anyone says about anything he does, as Umberto will do what he wants to do; it has been that way since he was 11 years old.

Since their wedding, Umberto and Anna have both suffered significant health problems. Anna has survived breast cancer and a hip replacement. Umberto had a stroke which remained undiagnosed for some time and had an operation on his hands at Queensland's Gold Coast. For a long time, he also suffered from an unknown illness, initially thought to be Ross River fever, although this was not proven.

It is a fact that people you know will pass away, and that even though we all know it, it is still unexpected and can happen in the most tragic of ways. Umberto and Anna had such an experience with their friends, Tony and Angela. During a holiday together in Mexico, they were at their hotel relaxing in their hotel rooms, having arranged to meet at a particular time. While Umberto and Anna were getting ready for dinner, they received a telephone call from Tony saying Angela was feeling sick. They rushed to their room and found Angela sitting on the bed. She looked at Umberto and said, "Umberto, I'm dying, I'm dying".

Angela deteriorated quickly, and in just a few minutes, she passed away in Umberto's arms. Tony stood by helplessly and in shock as Angela lay lifeless on the floor. After they called for help, Tony clumsily prepared documentation while they were waiting for the ambulance. They were all in shock by the time Angela was taken to the local morgue and a few days later was repatriated to Canada. The following week, on the day of Angela's funeral, Tony also passed away.

However, life went on, and Umberto and Anna continued travelling the world. In late 2006, they toured

A Better Life

Italy and England to catch up with Anna's son, Tony and his wife, Sharon, who had gone to see their daughter who was studying in England. They also spent three months in Italy with Anna travelling to Florence to visit with her family, while Umberto went to Sezze to visit with his family.

Following their holiday, Umberto and Anna agreed they would travel back and forth between Canada and Townsville every six months. However, a series of events led to a third person coming into their lives. Umberto had a grandson with whom he had lost contact, and after many years of searching, found him and invited him to visit with them in 2009 and shortly after was granted guardianship. His grandson went on to complete his high school education and a university degree. Umberto feels his grandson has also been given a second chance at a better life and considers he has grown up enough to be on his own and to make the best of what he has.

Umberto's older brother, Ercole, to this day, still lives on his farm in Millaroo. Ercole's sons also live on a farm in Millaroo. Ercole also has two other children, both girls, one of whom passed away. Ercole, at 87 years young, still travels the 320 kilometres round trip from Millaroo to Townsville once or twice a week to visit Umberto, doctors, and friends. Umberto's younger brother, Ezio, lives in Italy on the family land, but in a different house, and works 4,000m2 of farming land with hired labour.

Having opportunities in life to change and divert energy into a different path is always there for the taking. For Umberto, there have been many opportunities that he has embraced without hesitation. Meeting Anna has meant everything to Umberto, and he feels genuinely grateful for her being in his life.

Having close friends like Mick and Joe has been an incredibly rewarding experience and something he will always remember. Being with their friend Angela who passed away unexpectedly, and then her husband Tony when he passed away, was an incredibly tough time, as it would be in any relationship. However, Umberto and Anna worked through these tragedies together. There is also no doubt that Umberto has survived the most terrible times in history. It is no wonder that he has always and continues to look forward to a better life.

CHAPTER 15

A Better Life

UMBERTO IS AN ORDINARY man who has lived an extraordinary life. He is always making plans and still has dreams. Some would think there is nothing left in life for Umberto to achieve. However, Umberto lives life outside the square of what some people think he should do, especially for his age. Umberto is still active and manages his property portfolio. And he knows that what's next on the drawing board is up for criticism and does not care what others think.

He recently bought two residential properties next door to each other. He had the vision to build a four-unit building development spanning the two properties and to live in one of the units. Some say he is stupid to have such a plan at his age. However, he is not inclined to change his mind if he believes it is the right business decision.

In the planning stages for this property, his architect drew up the plans that were to include bathroom facilities attached to each of 15 bedrooms in the four-unit property. He sweated over this for many weeks, and after much discussion with his architect settled on a final plan that included bathroom facilities and other things he wanted.

However, after many months of planning and quotations, he accepted the cost of building the property was prohibitive. He is now looking to sell the land and move onto his next project.

In describing the person that Umberto is, I would say he is a determined, stubborn, compassionate and generous man who has always dreamt of a better life. He is the type of person who does not do anything wrong and if he does, is very sensitive to the impact and effect of the wrongdoing. By way of example, there is an incident that has troubled him for more than 50 years. It happened when he was driving a truck from Millaroo to Townsville transporting corn. Umberto was pulled over by a highway police patrol car for no reason, and while he felt quite stressed about it and nothing came of the incident, since then he has not slept well.

He has tried many different types of medication to help him sleep. Most people his age take some sort of drugs, but there is none that he has found suitable. Instead, he takes various herbs that help him with restful sleep and keep him healthy. In particular, he swears by two herbs; Ginkgo Biloba for blood circulation and Burdock Root, which reduces swelling in ankles. He also grows aloe vera for infections and applies it topically to burns, and makes a herbal concoction from it, which he believes is excellent.

About his natural medication, Umberto says, "There is nothing better that!"

In one discussion with Umberto, I asked him if he wanted people to know one thing about his life, what would it be? What does he want to be his legacy? I was not ready for his reply when he said, "They can say anything. Some will tell you I was a mean man. Others might say I looked after my money. For example, with my current project, I would have done anything, but the market is not right, so I have put the project on hold." They would also say, "He was a great man and put up with a lot of difficulties, but he succeeded."

I don't believe that Umberto is a mean man. I do think Umberto wants to be remembered for the person that he is, for what he has been through, and what he has achieved.

Over the years, there have been a lot of people Umberto has helped and others he chose not to help for one reason or another. Umberto has always dreamt of a better life and never let anyone or anything get in his way. He has worked incredibly hard all his life, and he wants people to remember what it was like for the early immigrants to Australia.

Looking back to the early days of arriving in Australia, Umberto felt angry at the treatment he received and about the promises made by the government. He does feel there was discrimination at a personal level at times, simply because he is Italian.

He has lived most of his life in Australia on a farm before diversifying and going into construction. Building his property portfolio has been exciting and encouraging, as he could rely on what he had already done.

In his business life, there were two significant events that he considers were the worst for him. The first in 1961 when he failed to sell his tobacco crop and subsequently burnt it to the ground. The other major event in his business life was in 1964 when he was refused a sugar cane permit which nearly sent him bankrupt. At the time, he had no way of addressing the issues and could do nothing to resolve them. However, he stood up for his principles as best he could to demonstrate what it meant to him.

Umberto will never stop thinking about a better life. He describes himself as unpredictable and can change projects or an idea very quickly and go from one thing to another, mainly if he sees a better way to do something.

Umberto can be a very generous, understanding, and compassionate man, who can be friends with anyone who wants to be friends, although his trust is hard-won. He has never hated anyone, including his first wife, Victoria.

These days, what is on his mind is his beautiful wife, Anna. He recently decided to stay in Australia while Anna returned to Canada to be with her family. Umberto understands that others may see him as being a very selfish and stupid person for not wanting to spend his twilight years with Anna. Each time he travels to Canada, he knows a decision must be made on whether he returns to Australia and that it will be a difficult one. Life goes on, albeit in different ways.

***

AFTERWORD

Early in 2019, Anna returned to Canada for health reasons. Umberto still lives in Townsville and speaks with Anna every week.

CHAPTER 16

Italians in Australia

ITALIAN IMMIGRATION TO AUSTRALIA began at around the same time as Captain Cook's discovery in 1770. On the Endeavour were two Italian men and a convict. Italian migrants also came here as free settlers, but there was no real Italian community until the 1850s. This was at the time of the gold rushes when immigrants from many countries, including Italy, came to Australia attracted by dreams of wealth and gold.

In the late 1800s, Italian migrants moved to the sugar cane fields of North Queensland as indentured workers. Conditions were harsh and wages low, with the workers enduring long working hours in almost unbearable heat.

There were Italians who migrated in the 1920s, but the most significant numbers came after the Second World War when economic conditions were terrible worldwide but considered better in Australia than in Italy. The Italians lived and worked in cities, started wineries, farmed tobacco, and cut sugar cane, influencing and forever changing Australian life and culture.

In the 1940s, many Italians were employers as pre-war settlers were often small farmers and shopkeepers. During the 1950s, many Italian families arrived although some men came without their families to find work before sending for the family to come later. Single men migrated on two-year contracts under the sponsorship of the federal government which made an imbalance of the sexes worse by the small-mindedness of the community and aversion by local young women towards Italian men.

In the early post-war years, Italian families were significantly affected by policies on family reunion, as it was controlled to prevent too high an immigrant intake.

From the 1950s to the 1970s, community formation and culture played a significant role in helping people deal with the consequences of assimilation policies and community attitudes. In general, non-English speaking immigrants did not know their rights and were often discriminated against by banks when they applied for loans. As a result, they started their small businesses with little information and few resources.

In contrast to the 1940s, by 1986 there were more Italian men working as employees and only a small number working as employers or being self-employed.

In today's Australian society, it is hard to remember there was a time before Italian food was part of our weekly dinner menus. There was a time when garlic was unknown, that olive oil was only available from chemists, that bread was cut in thin square slices, that cheese came in silver paper, that pasta was not a familiar dish, that wine was a foreign beverage, and tea was far more popular than coffee. Where once Italian restaurants were non-existent, they are now everywhere, and coffee is now an Australian favourite beverage.

A Better Life

The family (La Famiglia) is the most crucial aspect of an Italian person's life. There is no doubt the family provides emotional and economic support and often forms the basis of their social circles. Although the fast-paced, twenty-first-century life has changed the dynamic of the Italian family, relationships remain incredibly close.

Italian culture has a deep focus on relationships, with socialisation important on both a formal and informal level. Italians are generally effusive in their public behaviour with a great deal of public embracing and kissing upon greeting people. Open spaces and taking a stroll in the late afternoon play a significant role in socialisation, allowing people to mingle, catch up with friends and hear the latest news.

Food in daily life is also a means of establishing and maintaining ties among family and friends. It is also a lovely tradition that anyone who enters an Italian home is offered food and drink.

Children are indulged when young, and as they grow are expected to obey their parents, contribute to the household and are trained to be loyal to the family. Italian parents generally hold authority over their children throughout their lives, and although they may seek independence, they tend to stay at home for years into their adulthood. There is a deep respect for older family members who, in turn, are dedicated to their children and grandchildren.

From a religious perspective, most Italians are of the Roman Catholic faith. They generally believe in life after death in which the good are rewarded, and the evil is punished. Rome, or more precisely, the Vatican City, is the centre of the Roman Catholic religion.

In today's Australia, multicultural policies embrace many cultures from across the world. In terms of community, people of Italian heritage are the third largest ethnic group, with Italian the third most spoken language.

REFERENCES

I would like to thank the following authors, companies, independent organisations and government departments, and to note their work for their research, which has been referenced in the following chapters:

Chapter 1 – Life in Italy

Encyclopaedia Britannica, Latina, Italy; The Editors of Encyclopaedia Britannica; last updated: 6-9-2011

Chapter 2 - The war years

http://www.history.com/topics/great-depression

http://www.historylearningsite.co.uk/modern-world-history-1918-to-1980/italy-1900-to-1939/the-economy-in-fascist-italy/

https://www.reference.com/history/were-causes-effects-world-war-ii-9fcd2def289c9b68?aq=Effect+of+World+War+II&qo=exploreArticles, 'What Were the Causes and Effects of World War II?'

https://www.reference.com/history/did-world-war-ii-begin-969de34b95aa4db, 'How did World War II begin.'

https://www.reference.com/history/role-did-italy-play-world-war-ii-a09a72f30eea70df, 'What role did Italy play in World War II.'

Chapter 3 - Thoughts of a better life

http://www.australia.gov.au/about-australia/australian-story/great-depression

Australian migrant ships 1946–1977, 2006, Plowman, Peter, Chiswick Publications Pty Ltd, NSW, Australia

https://victoriancollections.net.au/items/52e791312162ef1
5b039b59e

Chapter 4 - The lucky country
http://www.bonegilla.com.au

https://www.fremantlemarkets.com.au/history

Chapter 5 - Catching rabbits
http://panique.com.au/trishansoz/animals/rabbit-australian.html

https://labourhistorymelbourne.org/the-rabbit-industry/

http://www.nma.gov.au/online_features/defining_moments/featured/rabbits_introduced

https://labourhistorymelbourne.org/the-rabbit-industry/

Chapter 6 – Cutting cane
https://www.daf.qld.gov.au/plants/field-crops-and-pastures/sugar

http://www.sugarmuseum.com.au/the-history-of-the-sugar-industry/

Chapter 7 - Farming life at Millaroo
https://en.wikipedia.org/wiki/Millaroo,_Queensland#History

https://trove.nla.gov.au/people/1474873

Chapter 8 - Growing tobacco
http://www.health.gov.au/internet/main/publishing.nsf/content/tobacco-kff, Department of Health, Queensland Government

http://www.tobaccoinaustralia.org.au/10-8-the-tobacco-growing-industry, The Cancer Council

Chapter 10 - Family
http://narrative.ly/the-disappearing-nuns-of-italy/
https://anunslife.org

Chapter 11 Losing Bruno
https://www.healthdirect.gov.au/tetanus

Chapter 16 - Italians in Australia
Encyclopaedia Britannica, Latina, Italy; The Editors of Encyclopedia Britannica

https://www.lifeinitaly.com/heritage/italians-in-australia

https://www.everyculture.com/Ge-It/Italy.html

https://culturalatlas.sbs.com.au/italian-culture/italians-in-australia

https://aifs.gov.au/publications/families-and-cultural-diversity-australia/7-italian-australian-family-transformation

ABOUT THE AUTHOR

Karen Guest is a writer with an interest in biographies. She first met Umberto several years ago, when he and his wife Anna, were visiting with her partner's family. Karen was intrigued by the story of a young boy in war-torn Italy who emigrated to Australia in search of a better life. Umberto's story is about persistence, being brave and determined, and triumph over adversity. His story is a personal journey about one boy's dream for a better life.

www.ingramcontent.com/pod-product-compliance
Lightning Source LLC
Chambersburg PA
CBHW030440010526
44118CB00011B/723